It's all in the

Cards

Chita St. Lawrence

A Perigee Book

A Perigee Book
Published by The Berkley Publishing Group
A member of Penguin Putnam Inc.
375 Hudson Street
New York, New York 10014

Copyright © 1999 by Chita Surowiecky
Cover design by Charles Björklund
Cover art by Catherine Stine
Book design by Lisa Stokes

First edition: January 1999

Published simultaneously in Canada.

The Penguin Putnam Inc. World Wide Web site address is
http://www.penguinputnam.com

Library of Congress Cataloging-in-Publication Data

St. Lawrence, Chita.
     It's all in the cards / Chita St. Lawrence. — 1st ed.
          p.   cm.
     ISBN 0-399-52494-0
     1. Fortune-telling by cards.   I. Title.
     BF 1878.S75   1999   98-40573
     133.3'242—dc21   CIP
Printed in the United States of America

10   9   8   7   6   5   4   3   2

Contents

Preface

*M*an's curiosity about tomorrow is probably as old as the human race itself. It would be safe to assume that from the dawn of time, man wanted to know the outcome of the upcoming battle, the success of the next hunt, the result of the trip he intended to embark on, and the effect of any and all events in his life.

Enterprising shamans, wizards, astrologers, and charlatans of all kinds, some of them believing in their own powers, took advantage of this human weakness, invented different methods of predicting the future, and used their "powers" not only for personal gain, but often as an instrument of control over the believers.

From the chicken bones thrown on the dirt floor of the cave to present-day psychics and fortune-tellers, predicting the future was a big business. Trying to glimpse the future is part of our everyday lives. We all read our horoscope in the newspapers. We turn on the TV just to hear the meteorologist predict the weather for the next five days. We try to guess the outcome of a football match. We invest our hard-earned money guided by the predictions of the stock market analysts.

This curiosity seems universal, and so does belief in horoscopes, palmistry, or card reading. Today we take these predictions with a grain of salt, and marvel if they come true.

Is it any wonder then that so many people today find, if nothing else, entertainment in card reading? They'll have their cards read "for fun," not believing in the predictions.

It was different when the Gypsies emerged in Europe during the tenth century A.D. and began to roam the land as horse traders, peddlers, and musicians. Gypsy women gained a reputation as healers and palmists. Some of them would throw a handful of beans into a tambourine and be able to tell the customer what he or she wanted to know. With the development of Tarot in the fourteenth century, they also became proficient in the art of reading those cards.

They mostly read futures at the carnivals and country fairs, but in the rural areas they would go from farm to farm, where the peasant women, who would not part with a coin even if they had one, readily paid with a chicken, a sausage, a slab of bacon, or a loaf of bread for having their palm read or fortune told.

As might be expected, the peasant woman would seldom confess to having her fortune told, so many Gypsy women when found with those provisions would be accused of thievery. This is not to say that Gypsies didn't occasionally steal a chicken or piglet from the backyard, some fruit from the orchard, a loaf of bread or a meat pie cooling on the windowsill, or even some clothing from the wash line. However, Gypsies were often unjustly blamed for many thefts committed during their stay in proximity of the scene of the crime.

The Gypsies were especially persecuted for stealing and maiming children in order to make beggars of them. The horrifying truth is that unwanted children, bastards and babies born deformed, were often given to the Gypsies by the citizens who wanted to hide those children from the eyes of polite society. The Gypsies were usually paid handsomely for the task of getting rid of those children.

Many of those babies died from the lack of mother's milk and the unsanitary conditions of a Gypsy camp, which allowed many diseases to take their toll. Those who survived were raised by the Gypsies as their own and trained in the nomadic way of life. That's why one could come across a blond, blue-eyed fortune teller. The deformed babies that survived infancy often became beggars because it was the only practical way for them to make a living. Female children were also instructed in the art of palmistry and card reading, which is not so simple as you may think. It takes years of learning and practice. Understandably, not every Gypsy girl grew up to become a fortune-teller.

Traditionally, only women could become palmists and card readers. They have something men lack, a special insight—today we call it "a woman's intuition"—which is considered the most important factor of fortune-telling.

Gypsy girls started learning the skills of palmistry and card reading at the age of twelve, usually with the onset of puberty. For several years, they learned to memorize the lines of the palms and the meaning of each card and how to interpret the layout of those cards from their mothers.

By observing other women of the tribe, they also learned how to ask prying questions and how, by connecting the answers to the card, the women were able to tell the customer what the customer wanted to know. It was also very important for a fortune-teller to understand body language. Every move, every gasp, every spontaneous gesture made by the Principal (the person whose fortune was being forecast) could be a valuable clue to render a satisfactory interpretation of the layout of the cards.

After mastering the basics of palmistry and card reading, a card reader would start using her own feelings (intuition, psychic powers, that special inner insight) on how to interpret what she saw.

Highly perceptive women became well known for their ability to accurately foretell the future. So the saying "It's all in the cards" only depends on the proficiency of the interpreter of the layouts.

There is no one established method of card reading, though similarities may exist. After learning the basics, a Gypsy woman would develop her own method and then teach it to her daughters, who, in turn, would also slightly change the method and then pass it on to the next generation.

Because the Gypsies never kept any records, I am convinced that much valuable and interesting knowledge has been lost. Over the years many different methods of reading cards were developed by enterprising women, who, not being of Gypsy origin, didn't have the basic training.

The method of card reading described in this book was developed, in the course of more than a hundred years, by five generations of Russian Gypsy women and was preserved due to the special circumstances of their lives.

It all began with Masha, songstress and dancer; it was carried on and further developed by her daughter Katya and then by her granddaughter Olya. Katya and Olya didn't sing or dance, but they made a lucrative enterprise of fortune telling. Not because they charged high fees, but because they never asked for any. The wealthy and the nobility, not wanting to be thought cheap, paid by discreetly leaving generous amounts of currency or gold on the table.

Olya's daughter, Tasha (short for Natasha), was not only beautiful, but an exceptionally talented singer and dancer. When she fell in love with a man who could not marry her, she left the stage. Her rich protector allowed her to live comfortably, yet she spent many years reading cards and perfecting the method of detailed reading. The method and set of skills was passed on to her daughter, Zina—the same method I am using today completely in its integrity.

Introduction

In Russia, Gypsies appeared in small groups, presumably during the reign of Catherine the Great. It is believed that one of Catherine's favorites, Count Alexis Orlov, imported the first Gypsy orchestra and choir from Moldavia. Others followed. Because of the long, bitter Russian winters, many Gypsies abandoned their wanderings and settled in Moscow, St. Petersburg, Kiev, and other large cities. They sang and danced in public houses.

The exotic qualities of Gypsy music—joyful exultation, sad and mournful, melancholy and gay at the same time— blended harmoniously with Russian melodies and folk songs and evolved into a special genre of Russian Gypsy music, popular today the world over.

Gypsy songs, such as "Two Guitars Behind the Wall," "My Campfire in the Dusk," and especially "Otchi Tchorniya (Black Eyes)," became very popular and integrated easily into Russian culture.

Catherine the Great herself was known to visit the "Red Pub" in St. Petersburg, accompanied by her "favorite" of the moment. She especially loved the romantic atmosphere during *Bielie Nochi* (White Nights), that transformed night into day.

After the victory over Napoleon and the return of peace, the nobility and rich citizens of Moscow and St. Petersburg entertained lavishly in their palatial homes. It was customary to have a group of Gypsies perform during those feasts.

For more than a hundred years, nightlife without Gypsy music was unthinkable. Several generations of prominent artists, composers, and writers listened to Gypsy songs, enjoyed their dances, and admired their rich and colorful costumes.

The great Russian poet Alexander Pushkin even spent a month in Moldavia, living in a Gypsy caravan. His romantic poem "Gypsies" and the well-known story "Queen of Spades" are testimonies of the impression Gypsies left on him. Count Leo Tolstoy, the great author and mystic, as a young officer fell passionately in love with Gypsy song. When Tolstoy retired to Yasnaya Polyana, he permitted Gypsies to camp on his property so that he could visit them and listen to their music.

It is safe to assume that both Pushkin and Tolstoy had their fortunes told. As writers, they wouldn't forgo the chance. Tolstoy also had close family ties with Gypsies. His uncle Theodor Tolstoy and his older brother, Nikolai, had both married Gypsy girls. So did quite a few other rich and noble men.

Nikolai Gogol, Ivan Turgenev, Fyodor Dostoyevsky, and Anton Chekhov, just to mention a few, appreciated Gypsy song. So did Mikhail Glinka, Nikolai Rimski-Korsakov, Modest Mussorgsky, and Igor Stravinsky. The Hungarian composer Franz Liszt, during his visit to Moscow, listened enthusiastically to Gypsy music and songs.

The Gypsies performed in restaurants but mostly sang and danced in *kabaks* (nightclubs), establishments where heavy drinking and some reckless gambling went uncensored.

In one of these establishments, frequented by dashing officers, wealthy landowners, aspiring artists, and well-known writers, a young Gypsy singer named Masha found herself in a dilemma, out of which developed the particular method of card reading described in this book.

Out of respect for the privacy of long-departed persons and any surviving descendants, the names of the people mentioned in this book are never given in full. And I am not using the full Russian forms of given names simply because they are a mouthful. (Masha's given name, for example, is more properly Maria Ivanovna.)

The Beginning:
Seven Cards Masha

*T*he year was 1820. In one of the kabaks *in the Black* River district of St. Petersburg, the principal singer in the Gypsy band performing there was a black-eyed, raven-haired beauty named Maria Ivanovna, or Masha for short. Her exotic beauty, pleasant voice, and graceful dancing earned her many admirers, who filled the house not only to gamble and drink, but to enjoy her performance.

One young man especially smitten with Masha was a talented artist, Sergei, who spent night after night sketching the patrons of the establishment, the musicians that performed there, and especially Masha, the star of the group.

One evening, while resting between the songs, Masha was accosted by a group of revelers in their cups.

"Hey, Masha, read us the cards!"

"I don't know how," replied Masha, smiling.

"Oh, yes, you do. You are a Gypsy. All Gypsies read the cards."

"But I don't have any cards." Not smiling anymore, Masha was annoyed.

Tossing her a deck of playing cards, one drunk (and obnoxious) young man exclaimed, "Now you do!"

No matter how firmly Masha tried to resist, the man persisted.

Realizing it was futile to argue with the drunkard, Masha took the cards and, not without theatricality, started shuffling them. Trained in the traditional way of Tarot cards, and faced with the task of reading the ordinary playing cards, Masha was at a loss.

But not for long.

Like any other Gypsy, she wasn't averse to seizing the opportunity for making some extra money and she decided to make the best of the situation. Without hesitation, she told the pompous young man:

"Sit down and cut the cards."

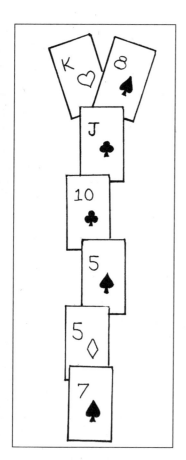

Drunk Young Man's Cards

Without looking at the cards, she collected them and started dealing them out, two by two, faceup, until the king of hearts turned up, paired with the eight of spades. She set both cards aside.

"What's that?" the young man asked.

"The king of hearts. It represents you. And the eight of spades means you will have a big argument."

In a column below that pair, Masha dealt out five more cards: the jack of clubs, the ten of clubs, the five of spades, the five of diamonds, and the seven of spades.

"You will argue with your friend about money," she said. "The argument will be fierce. You will not only lose that friendship but you will end up crying in despair."

The young man rose, threw some coins on the table, and mumbled, "I never cry."

After the group of young people left, Sergei, who had witnessed the whole incident from the next table, showed Masha the sketch he'd made of the seven cards she'd laid out on the table, and asked:

"Masha, would you tell me how you knew what to say?"

"Simple. I gave each card a meaning, according to what it reminded me of." She pointed to the individual cards as she started to explain them.

"The king of hearts was that young man, the eight of spades looked like a lot of angry words, the knight of clubs has a friendly face. The ten of clubs reminded me of spilled coins, the five of spades is such an empty card, it reminded me of a loss. The five of diamonds looked so friendly while the seven of spades definitely made me think of tears.

"As I looked at those cards, the words just came out of my mouth. I don't understand why. Anyhow, no harm done! When he sobers up, he'll forget all about what I told him tonight."

But the episode wasn't to be forgotten, not for a long time, if ever. A couple of weeks later, the same young man was caught cheating at cards. Trying to redeem himself, he challenged each of his accusers to a duel, which they all refused, declaring they would not fight with a lowlife.

Humiliated to the marrow of his bones, shunned by everybody, including his family, he left St. Petersburg for a remote province where his father had some properties and was never heard of again.

As word of her astonishingly accurate prophecy spread, Masha found herself besieged with demands for reading the cards. So, between songs and dances, Masha would oblige the customers by telling them what was "in the cards." Not all readings were special, yet most of them were surprisingly satisfactory. Once in a while, her predictions became memorable. They were always recorded by Sergei with a sketch and an explanation of the readings. He would also note the outcome of those readings, if they became known.

Masha sincerely believed that seven was the strongest number in the universe. Until the end of her days, she refused to read anything but seven-card layouts, which for the noisy and unruly crowd of the *kabak* was enough. And no matter how intricate the reading, it usually referred to only one event.

As the years went by, she became known as "Seven Cards Masha."

She also refused to read the cards to answer a specific question. To those requests she would answer, "It's all in the cards. I can only read them to you as they are laid out."

Only once did she break this rule. One persistent young man, known for his reckless ways, became rambunctious and verbally abusive after she refused to tell him when he was going to die.

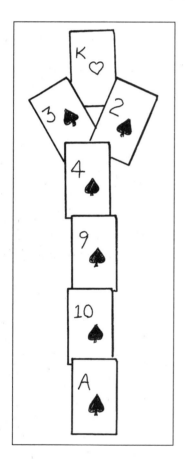

The Numbers 23 and 32

Advised by some sober patrons, Masha finally gave in. As usual, she dealt the cards until the king of hearts came up, followed by the three of spades. She set those two cards in the center of the table and told the man to randomly take out of the deck one more card and put it faceup next to the three of spades already in front of her. The card he drew was the two of spades. Masha added four more randomly selected cards below the first three. Astonished, she shook her head. Beside the two cards next to the Principal, the remaining four cards were also spades: the four of spades, nine of spades, ten of spades, and ace of spades. She indicated the two cards next to the royal card.

"Your black number is thirty-two."

"Oh, no, it's only twenty-three, you ignorant Gypsy! You can't even read numbers," exclaimed the young man sitting across from her, and seeing the cards in reverse.

Unabashed, Masha continued:

"But, first you will be torn apart by terrible sickness and suffer very much before you die."

Disgusted, he left, swearing, while his friends reassured him, "The stupid woman doesn't know what she is talking about."

Masha, shaking and in a fit of wrath, answered with a Gypsy curse. "May you drown in your own tears. May you rot in pain and your soul burn in hell."

For weeks to come, the whole episode was a laughing matter and subject of jokes to those who witnessed the reading. And then it happened. The young man fell off his horse and barely survived his injuries. The year was 1823. He lived as a paraplegic until 1832, when he died at the age of thirty-two.

His last words, according to those present at his deathbed, were "Damn Gypsy, she was right. My black number *is* thirty-two!"

Another memorable case Sergei recorded involved a dashing young officer, known to be a ladies' man. At the time of the card reading, he was involved in a scandalous affair with a married woman. The cards Masha laid out for him were the king of hearts, the six of spades, six of diamonds, six of clubs, six of hearts, the queen of hearts, and, finally, the ten of clubs.

"Sir! You have an arduous trip before you, at the end of which there is a young woman and lots of money awaiting you."

The young man, who was just falling in love again, interpreted it as a new conquest in love and a gain from gambling.

However, to his chagrin, because of the scandal he was involved in and by the influence of the elderly husband of the lady in question, he was banished to a remote garrison in the Caucasus. After some time, the news reached his friends that he had married a beautiful Georgian girl, who brought him an enormous dowry.

• • •

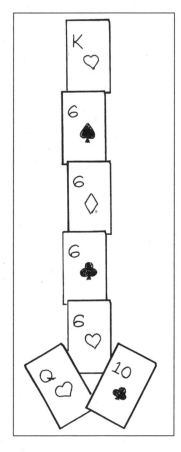

Dashing Young Officer's Cards

Mr. B was a respectable citizen. A member of a well-to-do family, he had considerable income. He wasn't a womanizer or a drinker. His only vice was that he gambled constantly. As a rich man, Mr. B could bet large sums of money and, like all gamblers, he won and he lost. Yet he always played within his limits, never entering in the games that would force him to write an IOU if he lost. If he won, he would be back the next day; if he lost, he would wait until his payday or his allowance from the family arrived. Unusual behavior for a consummate gambler, yet he was well liked for it.

Nothing indicated his unhappy end. His ruin, though it came through gambling, wasn't financial.

One evening after he was extremely lucky at cards, Mr. B asked Masha to read him what lay ahead.

At that time, he was about to marry a lovely young widow, to whom he had promised to stop gambling. Yet obviously he didn't take that promise seriously.

Masha laid out seven cards: king of hearts, two of spades, queen of hearts, five of spades, nine of hearts, seven of spades, and ace of spades.

Sergei, who was, as usual, sketching the scene, noticed Masha's hesitation and her somewhat vague interpretation. Later, Sergei asked, "What was really in those cards?"

"The breakup between him and his fiancée. Loss of love, lots of

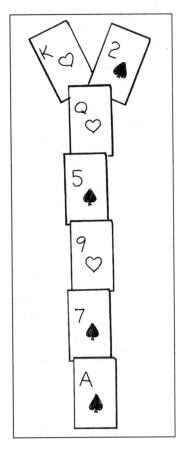

Mr. B

tears and death. As I see it, one of them is going to die with a broken heart."

Shortly thereafter, the widow called the wedding off. This was such a blow to Mr. B that he even stopped gambling. He tried to drown his sorrow in vodka to no avail. After the widow married somebody else, Mr. B was found dead by his own hand.

Masha had a little dog, who, incidentally, she believed to be the reincarnation of somebody she once knew. On her daily walks with her dog, Masha befriended a young governess of unusual beauty and sweet disposition. Though the girl spoke perfect Russian, her accent indicated her foreign origin. It turned out that the girl was English, from a good but impoverished family. She had taken her present position as a governess in order to escape an unwanted marriage her parents sought to impose on her. The letters she sent home from Russia went unanswered. Her employer treated her well, the children she cared for were good, and she loved Russia. Yet she ached after England and her family. Masha understood. They both were accepted by society but only halfway. One day, when the opportunity presented itself, Masha there and then laid seven cards out on a park bench. The seven cards Masha laid out were the queen of hearts, queen of clubs, five of diamonds, two of diamonds, king of hearts, six of hearts, and ten of diamonds.

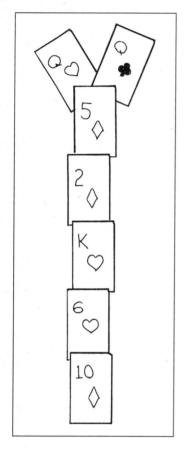

English Governess

"This is wonderful!" Masha exclaimed as she looked at them. "Through an older woman friend, you are going to meet a young man who is going to lead you to great happiness. I have never seen such cheerful cards before!"

"It's you!" replied the girl. "You are my only friend in this country."

"It is not me. I am just a Gypsy singer; I could never introduce you to any eligible bachelors."

However, a couple of weeks later, Sergei happened to be in the park with an old army buddy. Introductions followed. It was love at first sight between the governess and Sergei's army buddy. Two years of a romantic courtship passed before the lonely English governess became the happy wife of an adoring husband and the mistress of a country estate that reminded her of her beloved England.

Masha's last reading occurred one bleak, cold winter night shortly before her death. By now old, frail, and retired from a performing life, she lived with one of her daughters, Katya, in a small cottage on the outskirts of St. Petersburg. Almost at midnight, a heavily veiled lady, dressed all in black, arrived at the cottage and asked Masha for a reading.

Katya tried to explain that her mother didn't read cards anymore and, in any case, she read only for the patrons of the *kabak*. At the same time Katya, who never solicited business, hinted that she could give the woman a detailed reading instead.

Yet the lady wasn't interested in that; she insisted on having the seven cards reading done by Masha. Something in her voice prompted Masha to agree. As Masha laid out the first two cards, the mysterious woman gasped.

The card next to the queen of hearts (the Principal) was the seven of spades, representing tears. Next came the two of diamonds, followed by the nine of hearts and the queen of clubs, predicting a meeting with a loving older woman, whose funeral was predicted by the last two cards, the ace of spades and the nine of spades.

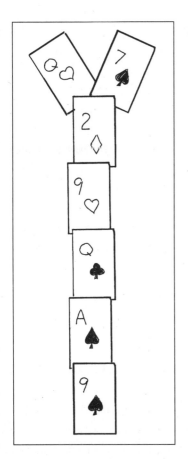

Masha's Last Reading

The lady listened attentively and then slowly slid off her chair onto the floor. She had fainted. When Katya lifted the woman's veil in order to give her a whiff of smelling salts, Masha gasped and fainted also.

Flabbergasted, Katya helped both women up. In the charged atmosphere of the room, she sensed a bond between the three of them. Suddenly the lady dropped to her knees in front of Masha.

"Mamotchka, forgive me!"

Masha also knelt and the two women embraced.

"I love you, mother," said the veiled woman.

"Bless you, my daughter," said the older. "It is good we meet again before I am gone."

All three women in the room suddenly realized that in the reading Masha had done for her daughter, she had predicted her own death.

A few weeks later, Masha was gone.

Sergei wasn't present at this reading, but he was able to make the sketch with all pertaining annotations after Katya related to him what had happened that night.

FROM MASHA TO ZINA TO ME

Sergei

I must take a moment to introduce Sergei to the reader and explain the role he played in the lives of Masha, Katya, and Olya, three of the five women in our story.

Count Sergei L. was a member of a very old family, whose noble roots could be traced to the time of the boyars, before the reign of Czar Peter the Great. He was a handsome young officer, who was about to marry a girl he'd loved since childhood, when Napoleon invaded Russia. He fought bravely against the invaders, was wounded twice, and returned home a decorated hero with a scarred face and without his left leg. His intended, a beautiful but shallow girl, refused to marry him. Embittered, he began to drink and gamble in the company of his fellow officers, some of them also crippled and mutilated from battle. He would perhaps have drunk himself to death if he hadn't met Masha and become devoted to her. It was not romantic love, but a sincere friendship that developed between them.

Watching her dance, listening to her songs, and sketching her and her cards became the purpose of his life. After Masha's demise, he stopped visiting the *kabaks*. He lived for many more years, managing the estate he inherited from his father. He also sired two sons by a peasant woman. When Sergei died he left all his sketches to Masha's youngest daughter, Katya.

The girl was illiterate and kept the colorful box with the sketches as a family heirloom. As such, the box passed from generation to generation until it came to Zinaida, an educated woman who was able to read those sketches and understand them.

Katya

Masha was married to the leader of her Gypsy band and they had three daughters and one son.

The oldest daughter, who was a great beauty, married a wealthy merchant, cut all ties with her Gypsy family, and became not only a highly respected matron in society, but a well-known patroness of art and benefactress of many charities.

The second daughter fell in love one summer with a young Gypsy passing through the area, married him, and joined his roaming tribe, thus resuming nomadic life and completely losing touch with her mother. Masha heard later through the Gypsy grapevine that her daughter settled in Spain and became a flamenco dancer.

Masha's third child, a son named Yakov, was very talented musically. He joined his father's band as a singer and balalaika player.

Katya, the youngest daughter, was still a small child when her two older sisters left, and she could barely remember them. But she dearly loved her brother Yakov and there was nothing she wouldn't do for him.

A sickly and lonely child, born with a club foot, Katya spent hours playing with the cards her mother gave her. She learned how to interpret them from Masha, but was bored with the seven-card layout and created her own system of the detailed reading. As time passed, she became proficient in the skill. She also developed a small idiosyncrasy.

Because the cards they used came from the gaming table of the *kabak,* Katya believed they had to be purified. She covered the table with a snow white cloth, spread the cards on it, lighted seven candles (most probably because her mother believed in the magic of the number seven), and left the cards that way for seven hours. She followed this routine for the rest of her life, even after she was able to buy new decks. After "liberating" the cards of all outside influences, Katya made sure that nobody touched them but herself and the person to whom she read.

One day Sergei took fourteen-year old Katya to his ailing mother, who wanted the cards read to her. The lady was very satisfied and the word spread rapidly. More and more, Katya would be summoned to the homes of fine ladies who wanted their fortunes told.

When Katya was sixteen, her brother Yakov and his wife were killed in a coach accident, leaving behind a two-year-old daughter, Olga—known as Olya.

Katya immediately took over complete care of the little girl, who soon started calling her Mama and, in time, everybody accepted little Olya as Katya's child. When the time came, Katya instructed Olya in the art of card reading.

Neither Katya nor Olya ever sang or danced. Not musically inclined, they both read cards and cared for the family. Olya married a blacksmith and Katya, who never married, had her hands full with numerous grandchildren.

Zina

It was Olya's daughter Tasha (Natasha) who became well known as a singer and dancer, and also as a card reader. She was so good at predicting the future that many thought her clairvoyant. Tasha was also a strikingly beautiful woman and had a long-standing liaison with a noble and very powerful man, with whom she had a daughter, Zina (Zinaida).

The man was a widower, childless in his marriage and crazy about his "Tziganotchka" ("Little Gypsy," the nickname he gave to Zina). He paid for a governess to educate Zina, but didn't forbid Tasha to teach her card reading. He only forbade Zina to do it in public and for money. When she married a nobleman and became a countess, he provided her with a rich dowry and a substantial annuity. Thus, he unofficially acknowledged Zina as his child.

Yet Fate wasn't kind to Zina. When World War I broke out, her husband was killed on the German front. During the Bolshevik Revolution of 1917, she joined the White Army as a volunteer nurse and, after their defeat, she retreated with them, first to Galipoli, then to Bulgaria and finally to the Kingdom of Serb, Croat and Sloven. Like most of the nurses and officers in the White Army, Zina was highly educated but without practical skills. Unable to find any kind of employment, she decided to break the promise given to her father years ago and began reading fortunes, both in the cards and on the palm. Officially she was Zinaida Petrovna; her numerous friends nicknamed her "the Gypsy Countess." For more than twenty years she made a modest living as a fortune teller.

During the housing shortage of World War II, Zina rented a room in her home in Sarajevo to a young nurse from the nearby hospital. The two women became very close. Zina, who was childless, loved the young nurse as if she were her own daughter.

During the long hours of the blackouts, with a curfew keeping them home at night, the Gypsy Countess would read the cards to the young nurse or reminisce about life in Old Russia and what she knew about Masha, Katya, Olya, and her own mother, Tasha.

The readings' effect was relaxing when one was stressed, soothing when one was troubled, reassuring when one was insecure. It was therapeutic during those uncertain years of German occupation. Sometimes a reading left one apprehensive, but we all know that life is not a bed of roses. Anything could happen, especially during wartime.

From those talks, Sergei's sketches, and the layout Zina showed her, the young nurse (who later married and became my mother) compiled a notebook of anecdotes and the method of card reading told to her by the Gypsy Countess, who died shortly before the end of World War II.

After the war ended, Mother fled Sarajevo ahead of the advancing troops of Marshal Tito. Packing her rucksack in a hurry, she also packed, without realizing it, the notebook with the instructions for card reading. She kept it, because it was one of the few things she brought from home. Today she believes it was *kismet*.

Me

One day, when I was a teenager, my girlfriends and I got involved in a discussion about fortune telling and Tarot. So when I came home from school, I found my mother in the kitchen and I asked for her permission to join my friends who were going the next day to visit a Gypsy woman and have their fortunes told.

Mom gave me a funny look and told me I didn't have to go to one because she could do it. She offered to read my cards right then and there. Agog with curiosity, I readily accepted. To my surprise, she opened one of the drawers and pulled out a regular deck of playing cards and started dealing them out on the kitchen table.

I was very skeptical at first, but as she started interpreting the layout, she revealed things I thought were my secrets (I was too young to know that mothers always know everything!). I became interested. She also forecast several events that intrigued me.

As days passed, and her predictions were being realized, I was impressed enough to ask her to teach me. She agreed; however, she made me promise I would never tell anybody that she read cards. And she never read for anybody but me.

The first thing she did was make me a copy of the Quick Card Suit Reference Table (shown on page 105). She showed me a seven-card layout and told me to start practicing and memorizing the meaning of the cards. While I did that, she spent several days translating her notes into English for my use.

When she handed me the copy she declared: "I'll help you with what I can, but basically you are on your own."

Throughout the years, not only did she help me on how to interpret the cards, but she accompanied the readings with the stories she heard from the Gypsy Countess.

Eventually I began interpreting the playing cards to my friends. We had lots of fun in the beginning, then we noticed how things were coming true. More and more predicted events were realized and I understood there is something unexplainable about the process.

For years, I've been reading the cards to my friends as well as to their acquaintances. They have all been so impressed with it that they suggested I write this book. After long deliberation I decided to put on paper all I know, so others can enjoy card reading as much as my friends and I do.

As my mother handed me the instructions with the words "you are on your own" so am I telling you:

Once you have read this book, and learn the basics, you will be on your own. Only you and your inner psyche will be able to read the cards successfully.

2

Interpreting the
52-Card Deck

Once in a while, in different countries and printed in different languages, a special deck of Gypsy fortune telling cards appears on the market.

In many of these new versions, each card in the deck carries an interpretation printed right on the face of the card. I have even seen quite a few of these new fortune-telling cards with not only pictures and words on them, but numbers printed on them as well.

I have found these numbered ones to be very clumsy. Worse, it is difficult to correlate one card with the next, especially when one has to find the several numbered cards listed on a given card to see if they lie anywhere near the card in question.

To top it off, these other versions have layouts that turn out to be even more complex than the Tarot's mul-tifarious layouts, which are notorious for that.

In my opinion, using these cards and complicated lay-outs is a waste of time and can try one's patience.

With Masha's interpretations of the standard fifty-two playing cards, readings are straightforward. One needn't "hunt" for matching or mismatching numbered cards floating somewhere about the layout.

In this section, the meaning of each card from the

four suits in a standard deck of fifty-two playing cards is identified and described. However, these interpretations are only starting points for the prediction. Because some adjoining cards can intensify or modify the meaning of any other cards, all adjoining cards in the layout should be taken into consideration before the final assessment is made. Once each card in the layout is identified and its meaning recognized, the cards are then read and interpreted collectively to form a clearer overall picture of the reading.

Several cards have straightforward definitions, yet the Reader must take care to regard such "simple" cards in all possible angles.

For example, the nine of hearts stands for love. Coupled with the two of hearts, its meaning expands to passionate love. Again, the Reader must examine the surrounding cards to determine whether this emotion is aimed at a person, the home, a job, or a trip.

Remember, the simpler a card's definition, the more powerful it is in interpretation.

To distinguish the roles of people present at a reading, I shall refer to the person whose fortune is to be read as the **Principal,** and the person who lays out the cards as the **Reader.** All others are kibitzers.

It is not known which deck of cards was given to Masha for the memorable reading that began the chain of events in our story. We can reasonably guess it was the deck of cards used for the game "rouge et noir," which was very popular at the time (the post-Napoleonic era).

Today, a standard deck of fifty-two playing cards is used. It is important, though, to discard jokers. The joker was added to the playing cards in America in the year 1865, almost fifty years after Masha established her rules.

We know for sure that it was Masha who divided the cards into major and minor groups. According to Sergei's sketches, the major cards in any of the four suits are the ace, six, seven, nine, ten, queen, and king. The minor cards in any of the four suits are the two, three, four, five, eight, and knight.

Sevens are the strongest, as they dominate emotions:

your thoughts	seven of diamonds
your tears	seven of spades
your jealousies	seven of hearts
your worries	seven of clubs

In the text that follows, you will notice that I use the term "royal" to identify the king, queen, or knight (jack). The Reader has the freedom to use the same term of reference or to refer to those cards as "face" cards.

It is worth mentioning an incident that occurred a couple of years before Masha's first reading, but which left a deep impression on her.

One evening, two drunken players placed their entire fortunes at stake in a one-card draw, in which each player draws a single card and the highest card wins. One man drew the ace of spades and lost when the other drew the queen of hearts. The loser, completely ruined, shot himself.

Hence the queen of hearts became Lady Luck and the ace of spades became the sign of death.

The Diamonds Suit

The square shape of the ace of diamonds reminded the Gypsy of a letter, so she associated it with news. All the cards in this suit are benevolent in themselves.

With the advance of technology, these cards represent news relayed in many different ways, including via e-mail and facsimile. Very often there is a telephone communication of some importance, or even a news received in a *tête-à-tête* conversation.

Don't forget that newspapers or television can give information that affects you personally: weather, flu epidemics, stock market fluctuations, accidents involving somebody you know, or a new medical research that could help you.

So when you think of news, don't limit your thoughts only to written words.

King of Diamonds

Father/son/young man. This card has three roles; the appropriate identification is clued by the surrounding cards. Usually this card represents the father, or father figure in a person's life; otherwise it represents a young man. Should the Principal be a parent, the royal card may represent a son, stepson, or a younger male who is regarded as a son. The card can also represent a very close friend who is considered a member of the family.

Queen of Diamonds

Young woman/daughter/mother. Just as with the king of diamonds, this card has three roles. The appropriate identification is clued by the surrounding cards. More than likely, this card represents the mother, or mother figure in a person's life. For a bachelor, this card could be a young woman. Should the Principal be a parent, the royal card may represent a daughter, stepdaughter, or a younger female who is regarded as a daughter.

Knight (Jack) of Diamonds

Expectation. Many times this is a hope or expectation borne for some time by the Principal or another person. It's especially meaningful when lying near or adjoining the representative card, the king or queen of diamonds, clubs, or spades. If it is not near any royal card, this card represents a general air of expectation. Depending on the surrounding cards, the knight of diamonds could be considered as a calm before the storm or a hopeful anticipation.

Ten of Diamonds

Happiness. Pure and simple in its meaning. Accompanying cards will identify its emotional link, which could be to love, the home, a job, a social gathering, or some relative.

Examples:
1. Next to the ten of clubs: unexpected wealth (windfall).
2. Next to the six of diamonds: vacation or a pleasant visit.
3. Next to any royal card: cause for rejoicing.
4. It could also represent a happy ending to any unpleasant situation.

Nine of Diamonds

Friendly surroundings/personal interest/ambition/advice. Demonstrating a supportive atmosphere in which the Principal's interest may be tied. This card could mollify any unfriendly cards that lie nearby.

Examples:
1. Next to a king of diamonds: personal ambition.
2. Next to the king of diamonds or the knight of clubs: friendly advice.
3. Next to a queen of diamonds: inner peace, contentment.

Eight of Diamonds

Socializing/pleasant small talk. A delightful card, signifying a festive atmosphere. This could be a cozy one-to-one chat (if accompanied by the king, queen, or knight of clubs) or a social gathering.

Examples:
1. Accompanied by several royal cards, especially if they are of the clubs or diamonds suit: a social gathering.
2. Next to the four of diamonds: think before making any social decision—for example, accepting a date or promising to help in organizing a social event or any volunteer work.
3. Surrounded by royals and the ten of diamonds: great social success.

Seven of Diamonds

Thoughts/wishful thinking/plans. This card is straightforward in its meaning. It indicates thoughts dwelling on matters of interest or, if accompanying cards enhance its meaning, a signal to think about a subject heretofore ignored.

Examples:
1. Next to the ten and the three of diamonds: the Principal's secret wish will come true.
2. Next to the nine of spades: the Principal is thinking about somebody's health.
3. Next to any royal card: the person represented by that card dominates your thoughts.

Six of Diamonds

Steps. This could be literal or figurative. There are measures to be taken that may involve a path or trip to achieve the next objective. The distances could be as short as across the room or to the door, sometimes as far as going across town or even overseas.

Examples:
1. Next to the eight and ten of diamonds: a pleasant group vacation.
2. Next to the three of diamonds: a successful enterprise.
3. Next to the ace of clubs (home): domestic harmony.

Five of Diamonds

Friendship. Good, supportive influences and beneficial relationship. Very close rapport if certain cards are found near this card—the four of hearts (nice gathering), for example, or any royal clubs.

Examples:
1. Next to the ace of diamonds: a friendly letter.
2. Next to the eight of clubs: friendly atmosphere at work.
3. Next to the knight of clubs and the seven of diamonds: a friend is supporting your plans.
4. It is a modifier to any unpleasantness.

Four of Diamonds

Decision/four corners. This card could be regarded in two ways. One is that it represents four directions, like a crossroads, intersection, or the four compass points. A person needs to consider which way to go—most likely it's decision time. The other interpretation is that it represents some element surrounding the person. This could be friendly and supportive (next to the three of diamonds) or it could be making the person feel surrounded by hostile forces (next to the four of spades). Once again, the elements of surrounding cards are to be taken into consideration. Guard against carelessness!

Examples:
1. Next to the four of spades: the Principal will have to make a decision against his or her will.
2. Next to the knight of spades: the Principal must decide how to handle a certain troublesome situation.
3. Accompanied by the four of clubs: the Principal will have to make a decision about a financial situation.

Three of Diamonds

◆ *Wish granted/objective achieved/success.* Caution with this one! The goal or desire attained may not be satisfying, yet change for the better will come in good time. Check the accompanying cards carefully.

Examples:
1. Accompanied by knight of diamonds: the expectation fulfilled.
2. Next to the five of clubs defines that card as the financial gain card.
3. Next to the ace of hearts: the Principal will conquer the love that at the moment seems impossible.
4. If the Principal is a woman and the three of diamonds is next to the knight of hearts, it means a child is in her future. She could become pregnant, marry into a ready-made family, or adopt a child.

Two of Diamonds

◆ *Meeting.* This represents a meeting between people; whether friendly or not would be determined by the accompanying cards.

Examples:

1. Next to the five of diamonds: friendly.
2. Next to the king, queen, or knight of spades: be cautious. The Principal could meet a two-faced person who means trouble.
3. Next to the eight of diamonds: there could be a public meeting or meeting a person or persons at a public place.

Ace of Diamonds

News. In the earlier days of communications, information usually came in the form of a letter or newspaper. As the ace of diamonds resembles a sheet of paper, it is a natural representation for news. In today's modern age, news could arrive through any media but the ace of diamonds consistently serves as its representative. The news may be good, bad, or indifferent, depending on the surrounding cards. Bad news itself is represented by the knight of spades (see page 28).

Examples:

1. Next to the ten of clubs: news of money.
2. Next to the ace of spades: news of death.
3. Next to the ten of spades: news of grave illness.
4. Next to the ten of diamonds: very happy news.
5. Next to the seven of hearts: news of rivalry.
6. Next to the nine of hearts: love letter.
7. Next to the six of spades: news of a failure.
8. Next to the six of hearts: the Principal will be asked for a date.

# The Spades Suit

The black color and sinister name of "spade" (in Latin, *spatha*) was associated with death and destruction.

King of Spades

Rival/widower. Considering the relationship this card has with the surrounding cards, the man could be a love or business rival. He may be a widower if surrounded by the ace of spades (death), the nine of spades (illness), or the ten of spades (great sorrow).

Examples:
1. Next to the nine of hearts: a love connection.
2. Next to the seven of clubs: a rival in business or on the job.
3. Next to any royal card: avoid the company of the person represented by that particular card.
4. Next to the card that represents the Principal: beware of a potential enemy.
5. Next to the seven of hearts: rival in love.

Queen of Spades

Rival/widow. Just like the king of spades, one must consider the relationship this card has with the surrounding cards. The woman may be a love or business rival. She may be a widow if surrounded by the ace, the nine, or the ten of spades.

Examples:
1. Next to the five of spades: expect treachery.
2. Next to the nine of clubs: she could be a love interest.
3. Next to the seven of clubs: definitely a rival at work.
4. Next to the seven of hearts: beware of a jealous and envious rival.

Knight (Jack) of Spades

♠ *Bad news/trouble.* Basically, it means a phase of time involving unpleasantness, the nature of which will be determined by the accompanying cards. Moreover, the news may come through a communication if the ace of diamonds (news) is present, or a person if a royal card accompanies this knight.

Examples:
1. Next to the nine of clubs: could be some trouble at work.
2. Next to the seven of hearts: infidelity.
3. Next to the eight of spades: somebody is spreading hateful rumors about you.

Ten of Spades

♠ *Great sorrow.* This is definitely a card of great sadness. By studying the accompanying cards the Reader should be able to determine under what circumstances this feeling will be evoked.

Examples:
1. Next to the six of spades: an extremely bad card. Be very careful, an accident may occur.
2. Next to the knight of spades: you have a mortal enemy.
3. Next to the seven of diamonds: hope against hope, for something that will never be.

Nine of Spades

♠ *Health problems/illness/funeral.* This could be taken as poor health, emotional stress, depression, or deterioration, as in undermining sources or causes. If by any clubs, another interpretation could be a flu bug going around the working environment or, more seriously, a deterioration of morale. The position of the inner spade determines the profundity of its meaning. Under specific, unusual circumstances the card represents the coffin or a funeral when coupled with the ace of spades.

Examples:
1. Coupled with the ace of spades: a funeral.
2. If the inner spade points toward any royal card, it presages an illness. If the inner spade points away from any royal card, the person will recuperate.
3. Next to the six of spades: drive carefully.

Eight of Spades

Argument. Clearly a disagreement of a serious nature. The degree of severity depends on accompanying cards. There will be unpleasant words, a verbal fight.

Examples:
1. Next to the eight of clubs: unpleasantness at work.
2. Next to the two of diamonds: unpleasant meeting.
3. Next to the two of clubs: the Principal will have a disagreement with a coworker.
4. Next to the ten of clubs: the Principal will fight about money. It would be an argument about unpaid bills or unnecessary expenses.

Seven of Spades

Tears. Usually signifying an event or circumstance causing sadness and weeping. Yet, if coupled with the ten of hearts (great joy), they could be tears of joy.

Six of Spades

♠ *Bad move* (faux pas)/*bad trip/unwise action*. It serves to alert the Principal to an upcoming event. This does not necessarily warn against travel, though. It could simply represent a troublesome spot on the road of life. If some physical distance is involved, as with other cards the distance is variable. In any case, it should be borne with fortitude. Such an experience, though troublesome, would most likely be temporary or of short duration in nature.

Examples:
1. Next to the eight of diamonds: the Principal should be careful not to commit a *faux pas* by saying something offensive or indiscreet.
2. Next to the four of hearts: avoid going to a party; it could be unpleasant.
3. Next to the eight of clubs: be careful about expressing your opinions at work.

Five of Spades

♠ *Loss*. Straightforward in its meaning. The kind of loss—for example, loss of people or friendship, job, or home—is very dependent on accompanying cards.

Examples:
1. Next to the five or the ten of clubs: financial loss.
2. Next to the five of diamonds or the knight of clubs: loss of a friendship.
3. Next to the nine of hearts: lost love.
4. Next to the six of spades: the Principal could get mugged.

Four of Spades

♠ *Doubtful/torn apart.* This card signifies upsetting indecision or separation in the strongest sense, possibly involuntary. The strength of emotion involved is akin to a person being drawn and quartered figuratively by surrounding forces. It involves unease and stress.

Examples:

1. Next to the ace of clubs: the Principal could be torn apart because of a family or job situation.
2. Next to the seven of hearts: jealousy is killing someone (adjoining card should explain whom).

Three of Spades

♠ *Cutoff/obstacle.* A versatile card, dependent on its position in the layout. A connection of any type is severed; for example, a relationship in business, love, friendship, or even a loss of communications could happen should the ace of diamonds (news) be involved.

Examples:

1. Next to the two of hearts: divorce; the breaking up of a relationship.
2. Next to any royal card: estrangement from the person that card represents.
3. Next to the six of spades: a trip (steps taken) with no return.
4. Next to the nine of diamonds: an obstacle to the Principal's ambition.

Two of Spades

Breakup/rift. A parting of the ways under unpleasant circumstances. Examine the companion card as well as its neighbors to determine the conditions and degree of separation.

Examples:

1. Any accompanying royal card indicates separation from the person that card represents.
2. Next to the ten of clubs: a disagreement about money/expenses.
3. Next to the ace of diamonds: a "Dear John" letter.
4. Next to the eight of clubs: danger of losing the job or income.

Ace of Spades

Tragedy. When the spade is upright (the stem is at the bottom) the card represents death; when upside down, it represents tragedy of very serious consequences. This is a very powerful card and its position among the other cards must be examined carefully to determine how it wields its influence.

Examples:

1. Next to the nine of spades and any royal: funeral of the person the royal represents.
2. Next to the five of diamonds: death of a friendship.
3. Next to the ten of clubs indicates bankruptcy; but if the ten of clubs is accompanied by the ten of diamonds or hearts, it represents inheritance.
4. Next to the nine of diamonds: a total failure of the Principal's personal ambition.

The Hearts Suit

It goes without saying that all heart cards are associated with love and romance! However, the love could be directed toward a friend, a relative, or even a pet.

Sometimes, it could mean love of sports or some hobby or even an inanimate object, like a favorite piece of jewelry or an antique or even an old sweater with sentimental value. Hearts can also modify the meaning of the more severe or unlucky cards.

King of Hearts

♥ *Principal/sweetheart.* If the Principal in a card reading is a gentleman, then this royal card represents him. If not, the other roles it plays follows.

Examples:
1. If the fortune is being read for the female Principal and the king of hearts is next to the ace of hearts, it represents her love interest.
2. Otherwise, it represents a nice man whose role in the layout is indicated by the adjoining cards.
3. If it is together with several other royal cards, it represents just a face in a crowd.

Queen of Hearts/Lady Luck

♥ *Principal/Sweetheart.* Like the king of hearts, this card has two roles. It identifies the female subject (the Principal) whose fortune is being read. When this card is drawn by a male Principal, the card represents his love interest.

Examples:
1. Another interpretation would be luck in financial matters if drawn by a male Principal and it is next to the ten of clubs.
2. Next to the eight of hearts: the lady is a flirt; don't take her seriously.
3. Next to the six of hearts: Lady Luck is accompanying the Principal in all enterprises.

Knight (Jack) of Hearts

New hope/child. After all, children are the hope of the future. This card represents sentiments close to a person's heart and/or mind that evoke warm or wistful memories. The knight also represents new hope.

Examples:
1. Paired with the king and queen of hearts: a child (no sex distinction).
2. Next to any numbered card: the child is approximately that age.
3. Next to any queen, this card represents a child; next to any king, a new hope.

Ten of Hearts

Great joy. This is a straightforward, very positive card representing great happiness and well-being.

Examples:
1. If next to the king and queen of hearts and followed by an ace of hearts, it is a possible wedding.
2. It is also a strong positive modifier when next to any unlucky card.

Nine of Hearts

Love/respect. The two rows of hearts on this card could be likened to a pair of hands holding the heart at the center. The position of surrounding cards might help define the potency of the emotion.

Examples:
1. Between the king and queen of hearts: an unbreakable bond between two lovers.
2. Next to the nine of spades: a heartbreak or a heartbreaking situation.
3. Next to the eight of clubs: the Principal is respected for his or her work.

Eight of Hearts

♥ *Friendly flirt.* This card represents someone who evokes good feelings with his or her attentions or a situation where friendly flirtation is exchanged.

Examples:
1. Modifier for the eight of spades (argument) and also for the seven of clubs (worries). Don't take the argument very seriously and don't worry too much.
2. Next to the knight of spades: the trouble is passing away.
3. Next to any royal card: the attitude of the person represented by that card shouldn't be taken very seriously.

Seven of Hearts

♥ *Jealousy/envy.* This potent emotion covers all phases of personal and material envy. Note the position of the center heart in relation to the Principal's card. The point of the inner heart could signify the sentiment being aimed against the Principal or by the Principal toward another person or a situation.

Examples:
1. Next to the king or queen of spades: somebody is envying you.

2. Next to the eight of spades: lovers' quarrel.
3. Next to the eight of clubs: somebody is trying to undermine the Principal's reputation.

Six of Hearts

Very nice trip or path. A pleasant passage or phase in life that augurs well-being and that may involve a very enjoyable venture. It usually represents short personal trips: dates, going to parties, visiting friends, or a trip to the mall. Any steps taken are pleasant.

Examples:
1. Next to the ace of hearts: a sentimental journey may be undertaken.
2. Next to the king of hearts or clubs: a date (for a woman).
3. Next to any of the queens: a date (for a man).

Five of Hearts

Small token/gift/little attention/a pleasant telephone call/surprise. This card is quite multifaceted in its interpretation, all of them good. Its temporary notation would signify a short period of time, say a few hours or days. For example, a nice evening out on the town or a weekend of visiting friends or relations. It's a phase of time pleasantly passed; if it is near a royal card, the person represented by that card is the cause of good times.

The gift and attention received could be unexpected or one causing great joy. It could be a holiday or birthday gift, a gift accompanied by a thank-you note, or a souvenir brought to the Principal by someone who made an unusual trip. It may be a small token of appreciation or just a gift because someone loves the Principal.

Four of Hearts

Nice gathering. A most pleasant event for any royal cards connected with this one. Just be aware that a rival may be present if a royal spade turns up near or is adjoining this card.

Examples:
1. Next to the ten of spades: could be a wake.
2. Paired with the ace of hearts: pleasant date.
3. Next to the nine of clubs: pleasant working conditions.

Three of Hearts

You and only you. All attention is focused on the Principal. The disposition of the focus depends upon the surrounding cards to tell whether it is personally or materially related.

Examples:
1. Next to the ten of diamonds: good health.
2. Next to the king or queen of hearts: that person loves and cares only about you.
3. Next to the ace of clubs: solid home life.
4. Also represents security when next to the cards of love, job, friendship, etc.

Two of Hearts

Passion. Strong feelings are represented by this card, sometimes good and positive, other times obsessive. If coupled with the seven of hearts (jealousy), the person must consider if he is generating the attitude himself or if it is directed toward him. With an eight of clubs (job), the person is passionate about his job or work. If spades are present, study the layout with care in order to be aware of all elements in the interpretation.

Examples:
1. Next to the ten of clubs, the person (this could be the Principal or any royal card) is obsessed with money matters.
2. Next to the eight of spades: a passionate argument. A third card could help determine what the argument is all about and if the third card is a royal, it could be the person with whom the argument will take place.

Ace of Hearts

Heart. Primarily involving the emotional aspect of the person rather than the physical body part. When the heart is upside down, all is not well. The Principal (or another person, if it's associated with another royal card) may have a sad or worried heart. The ace of hearts is open to further interpretation dependent on the adjoining card or surrounding layout. If connected to a royal card, consider it carefully in its position and how it relates to that person and the environmental forces (cards) surrounding it.

The Clubs Suit

When viewed upside down, the club reminded the Gypsy of a pawnshop's symbol,
dating back to medieval times, consisting of
three gold balls suspended outside the
shop's entrance. Thus, most of the clubs in
the suit would interpret various aspects tied
in with business, finances, or any enterprise
that involved money.

King of Clubs

Friendly older man/relation. This card usually represents a male friend of the Principal. If the card adjoins the ace of clubs (home), then this involves a male relation of the Principal.

Examples:
1. Next to the two of clubs: somebody at work in a higher position than the Principal.
2. Next to the nine of clubs: the boss.
3. Next to the king of hearts: very close, sincere friendship.
4. Depending on other adjoining cards, could also represent an older relative, father, uncle, or grandpa.

Queen of Clubs

Friendly older woman/relation. This card has a similar role to the king of clubs in that it represents a female friend of the Principal. Again, if the card adjoins the ace of clubs (home), then this is a female relation of the Principal. She could also be the boss.

Examples:
1. Next to the queen of hearts: very close, sincere friendship.
2. Next to the nine of spades and the five of hearts: could be a nurse or somebody who takes care of a sick person (not a doctor).
3. Together with the king of clubs: an elderly couple or grandparents.

Knight (Jack) of Clubs

Friend. A general representation of the Principal's friend or, if by the ace of clubs (home), this could be a younger relation.

Examples:
1. Next to the nine of diamonds: expect friendly advice.
2. Next to the ace of hearts: the Principal's best friend.
3. Next to any royal: the Principal can trust the person represented by that particular royal card.

Ten of Clubs

Money. An interesting card with many possibilities. Finances are the main concern here, whether an investment, expenditure, or earnings. This could involve personal or business matters. For example, if coupled with the five of hearts it could mean an expenditure of indulgence by the Principal for her own pleasure, from buying a bestseller to acquiring a personal accessory that was eyed for some time. If an additional card is the eight of diamonds (socializing/pleasant talk), it could be that the Principal will treat friends to a social gathering or a night out on the town or will throw a party.

Examples:
1. Next to the seven of hearts: somebody is envious of the Principal's success.
2. Next to the ten of spades: the Principal will get an inheritance.
3. Next to the five of clubs: financial difficulties.

Nine of Clubs

♣ *Business site/business enterprise.* Definitely a place where the environment is geared for business, be it an office or store or factory, or even a corner of your attic where you keep your computer (home office). This would be a physical location and its nature would be revealed by the cards around it.

Examples:
1. Next to the ten of diamonds: pleasantness at the workplace.
2. Next to the five of clubs: a possible raise.
3. Next to the seven of spades: unpleasant situation at work.
4. Next to the eight of clubs: possible promotion or raise in salary.

Eight of Clubs

♣ *Job/business talk.* Employment or another task or duty that has been, is being, or will be performed. It could indicate anything from a simple errand to full employment. Its position in layout will reveal its potential significance to the Principal.

Examples:
1. Next to the six of diamonds (step up): possibility of advancement.
2. Next to the three of diamonds: everything is okay at work.
3. Next to the four of spades: something is not *kosher* in the office.
4. Next to the seven of clubs: insecurity at work. You could lose your job.

Seven of Clubs

♣*Worries.* Self-explanatory in nature yet dependent on adjoining cards. If the other card is the ace of diamonds (letter), the news could be worrying in nature. There could be worry for lack of news if the three of spades is present as well. If any royal cards are present, there may be concern on behalf of that person or worries directed toward that person because of his or her actions. Check the layout for any nearby or adjoining business, love, monetary, or health cards for further clarification.

Examples:
1. Next to the ten of clubs: the Principal definitely worries about money.
2. Next to the seven of hearts: somebody's jealousy worries the Principal a lot.
3. Next to the ten of diamonds: you worry for nothing.
4. Next to the six of hearts: a trip to the Principal's place of worship could alleviate his or her worries.

Six of Clubs

♣*Any trip, steps, or measures taken in relation to business.* This card should be taken seriously.

Examples:
1. Next to the ace of clubs: could mean moving into another residence or changing jobs or even a position change within the same company.
2. Next to the six of spades: try to avoid or at least postpone the trip the Principal is planning in the near future.
3. Paired with the three of diamonds: the trip will be successful.

Five of Clubs

Gain or loss. It is a stock market card. This card can be baffling at first when gauged against the surrounding ones. The positive or negative interpretation of this card strongly relies on the influence of the others. If business situations are implied, the nature is of the venture's gain or loss, whether involving a job or a meeting.

Examples:
1. Next to the ten of clubs: it's monetary, like finding loose change, winning the lottery, perhaps losing a bet or making a poor investment.
2. Next to the eight of spades: a stalemated argument.

Four of Clubs

Financial insecurity/undecided business. This card signals a situation that may come to pass (or that even exists yet the Principal is not aware of it) that warrants caution and a great deal of thought, especially if it requires that he or she make a financial decision and act upon it.

The indecision could be about a major purchase: a car, a home, furniture, or an expensive piece of jewelry or clothing.

Example:
1. Next to the ace of clubs: the Principal could be contemplating a sale of some property.

Three of Clubs

Perseverance/hard work. Any dream can be fulfilled, any goal achieved with perseverance and hard work. The cards surrounding it should be explanatory.

Examples:
1. Next to the eight of clubs: the Principal should concentrate harder on his or her job.
2. Next to the six of clubs: hard work ahead.
3. Next to the three of diamonds: success. Perseverance pays.

Two of Clubs

♣*Business meeting.* Possible discussion of matters not pertaining to personal interest or emotion are taken into account. This may involve two or more people discussing such topics, like a meeting with the boss, lawyer, other business-oriented personnel.

Examples:
1. Next to the king of clubs: meeting with the boss.
2. Next to the four of clubs: meeting with your banker.
3. Next to the nine of spades: the Principal will meet with his or her doctor. The adjoining cards will explain whether the Principal is sick or will get a clean bill of health.

Ace of Clubs

♣*Home.* The card represents the residence, yet if it is tied in by other clubs, it could imply headquarters or a base of operations. If the club is upside down, there is trouble at home (or base) that the Principal may not be aware of—or if aware, should resolve as soon as possible. If the ace is upside down, and accompanied by other business-related cards, this indicates a reversal of fortune or prospect.

Examples:
1. Next to the two of diamonds: a visitor is coming.
2. Next to the six of hearts: a change for the better.

3. Next to the king of clubs: the Principal is "teacher's pet" (most probably well liked by the boss) or somebody higher up. It could also represent a person of great influence not related to the Principal's current job.

FOUR OF A KIND

When the cards turn up in pairs or in threes, they compliment, explain, or reinforce each other, according to the adjoining cards. When you have four of the same value they acquire special meaning, although still pertaining to what they usually represent. It goes without saying the other cards in the layout play very important roles in clarifying the interpretation.

Kings

When all four kings show up in the layout together, they represent a very strong group of men. Army, police, board of directors, a football team, or any other groups that are traditionally considered a group of men.

On the negative side, they could be a car full of hooligans or a neighborhood gang. Tread carefully and don't step on them; avoid arousing their ire, let alone their attention.

Queens

Four women grouped together could mean friends and family gathered for a baby or bridal shower.

They could represent the Principal's classmates, coworkers, or neighborhood klatch. It all depends on what the rest of the cards indicate. No matter what the adjoining cards indicate, this foursome is, in essence, harmless.

Knights (Jacks)

Here you have nothing but a bunch of kids. They could be rambunctious preschoolers or unruly teenagers. In any case, the Principal should beware of trouble and ought to learn how to handle toddlers, teenagers, and in-betweens.

Tens

Happiness, sorrow, joy and money. Happiness and joy will come through money. Sorrow indicates possible inheritance, but doesn't guarantee it. The ten of spades could represent difficulty in collecting some money due to the Principal. Or the Principal could hit the jackpot and suffer because of the demands the status of winner imposes upon him or her. Yet, it is the nicest foursome in the deck.

Nines

Definitely indicates a very busy life. The surrounding cards should explain the situation, or indicate on what phase of life to concentrate in that moment.

Eights

Some unusual happening in the Principal's social life. Again, pay close attention to the surrounding cards.

Sevens

Thoughts, tears, jealousy, worries. The Principal is a very emotional person. Advise him to control himself.

If those cards are next to any king or queen, the Principal will have to deal with a very, very emotional person.

And if they are next to the ace of spades, those emotions could become very dangerous.

Sixes

Two different meanings in the same direction. First, the Principal may contemplate a long trip. It can be a vacation or a move to a distant place. The journey will have its bad moments, but conclude satisfactorily.

Second, the idea of a long trip could represent the Principal's life's journey, with all its ups and downs.

Fives

A person close to the Principal is a devoted friend. Through thick and thin, good or bad, the Principal can always count on that person. This kind of devoted friendship is rare. When the Principal is blessed with it, he or she should cultivate it carefully.

Fours

The Principal has a problem, which he or she is doubtful can be solved. But a decision has to be made one way or another. If the four of spades is flanked by the four of diamonds and the four of hearts, the decision the Principal makes will be a wise one.

Threes

Success, obstacle, you and only you, perseverance. Only by perseverance and hard work can the Principal overcome the obstacle that is obstructing his or her success.

Twos

Meeting, rift, passion, business. A public meeting, be it political, at work, or at the PTA, will have heated discussions and disagreements.

Aces

News, tragedy, heart, home. News the Principal will receive, or has already received, will turn his or her life upside down. It will be very upsetting and he or she will, until it's all over with, be literally sick.

If, by any chance, this foursome is followed by the ten of diamonds, the trouble will be soon over.

3

Reading the Cards

*F*or the sake of clarity on which actions (shuffling, cut-ting, handling, and dealing out the cards) are done by whom, we will assume two people are involved in the reading of the playing cards (as opposed to the times the Reader interprets his or her own fortune).

The two participants, you will recall, are the Reader, the person who interprets the cards' layout, and the Principal, the person whose fortune is being read.

The Principal's representative card is either the queen of hearts or the king of hearts, depending on whether the Principal is a lady or a gentleman, respectively.

Without doubt, there will be occasions when you, the Reader, will wish to have your own fortune forecast. Hap-pily, the Reader can quite easily read and interpret her own cards and does not have to depend on another per-son to take on the role of the Reader.

In the event the Reader is casting her own fortune, she will carry out the same instructions for the Principal, as stated in the following section, so the reading will play out smoothly. Naturally, the Reader turned Principal will interpret her own cards with more depth and under-standing.

On the average, card readings interpret possibilities roughly four weeks into the future—that is, a month of days. After doing many readings over many years I've found the time frame to be consistent.

Several of my friends who consult astrology charts prefer to have readings done at the beginning or the end of a month (in anticipation of the oncoming weeks); other friends are quite satisfied with having readings conducted only once in a great while—say, quarterly or even seasonally.

After a brief explanation on how to prepare the playing cards and initiate the start of the readings, I will, in the sections that follow, describe three kinds of readings. Each description will be accompanied by an illustration to enhance your instruction on how the layouts are dealt out and constructed.

The layouts are:

1. The Quick Cut
2. The Short Reading
3. The Detailed Reading

The Reader will find the Quick Card Suit Reference Table, provided at the conclusion of this book (see page 105), to be a handy tool. Even the more experienced playing card Readers may wish to refer to it from time to time, to help jog their memories. All Readers will find it quite helpful, especially when a particular card can have different roles or interpretations. There will be occasions when a card's role, as a result of its proximity to the other cards, is not apparent or immediately recognized.

When the occasion arises that a card's role is not self-evident or conspicuous enough, as a result of its proximity to other cards, the Reader should refer to chapter 2 and look up that card's identity and possible interpretations when in combination with other cards.

STARTING OFF

A deck of 52 standard playing cards is used for all the layouts described in this book. Remember to omit the jokers, as these cards have no value or use in the layouts.

During a reading, all shuffling is done by the Principal, while drawing the cards for the layouts will be done by the Reader.

The one exception during the handling of the cards might occur when the Principal and Reader work together in drawing the cards during the final stages of the Short Reading. This action would only occur at the Principal's request, if he or she desired further explanation of the initial five-card layout.

The Principal starts off the reading by shuffling the cards in the manner he or she finds most comfortable. How the cards are shuffled is unimportant—it may be in the fashion of a Las Vegas dealer or of the Peanuts' Lucy van Pelt (she shuffles by tossing the cards into the air and then picking them up one by one!). As long as the cards are mixed thoroughly to provide a diverse layout and interesting reading.

While handling and shuffling the cards, the Principal is to relax and think about, but not heavily concentrate on, a subject that most interests him or her, or on the goal that he or she hopes to achieve in the near future. Interpretations are clearer when the thought is realistic and not a fantasy.

The Principal continues to mix the cards until he or she feels ready to start the reading.

The Principal will elect which reading to use. I've discovered that my friends prefer starting out with the Quick Cut, continuing with the Short Reading, and finishing with the Detailed Reading. So, in that popular order, you will find the instructions for each one in the following pages.

The seven-card reading is done, as far as I know, only by my mother when she does it for herself. Yet, I am including the instructions just in case you like the system and would like to use it yourself.

THE QUICK CUT

When ready, the Principal will place the deck upon a smooth surface, preferably a table, facedown. He or she will then cut, or split, the deck into two sections and place the top half of the deck faceup, beside the bottom half, on the table. (Figure 1a illustrates this maneuver.) This exposed card will be referred to as the inner card.

The Reader will then take the remaining half, currently resting facedown on the table, and flip the stack over to reveal its bottom card, which shall be referred to as the outer card. (The final appearance of the Quick Cut is illustrated in figure 1b.)

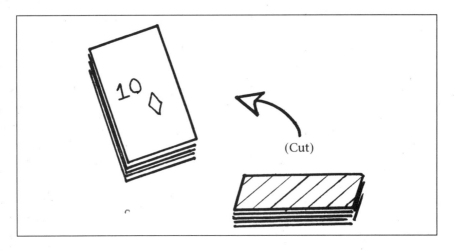

Figure 1a. Inner card revealed in top half of cut.

Thus, with the two halves' cards revealed, the Reader is ready to start the Quick Cut reading.

With reference to the first half's card (the group exposed by the Principal), the Reader will be able to determine whether or not the Principal's goal or wish will be achieved. If the exposed inner card is red, the prospects are favorable.

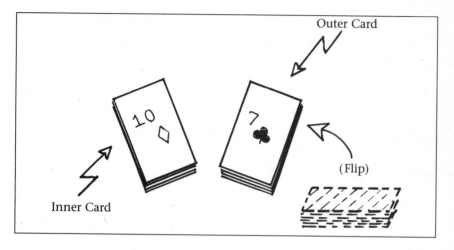

Figure 1b. Outer card revealed in bottom half of cut.

If the inner card is black, the attainment of that goal is blocked. (Remember to reassure the Principal that this is only a temporary impediment. At the most, the delay would be for approximately four weeks, give or take a few days.)

Knowing whether or not the goal will be achieved, or the wish granted, the Reader proceeds to the next step.

In addition to noting the color of the inner card, the card's identity, or representation, is determined. Then the Reader may establish what circumstances will govern the goal's atmosphere or how the realization of the wish will be influenced.

If the card happens to be a royal, the card may identify the type of person connected with the Principal's goal or wish, and how that person's role will influence the Principal's attainment of (or failure to attain) that goal, or the fruition (or unfulfillment) of his or her wish.

The Reader's next step is to link the two cards' representations by identifying their roles and interrelating them. By following this action, a fuller interpretation may be achieved.

A knowledgeable Reader will look at both cards and read them in two directions to help confirm his or her initial interpretation of the cards. That is, the Reader will link the meaning of the first half's card to the second half's in one direction, then interpret their roles the other way around by linking the two cards' meanings in reverse order.

If any inconsistencies are revealed, the Reader is recommended to reexamine the cards and attempt an interpretation once more.

With practice, and from experience gained by reading cards from all vantage points, the true interpretation will be intuitively recognized by the Reader.

Once the cards have been interpreted, this information could help the Principal prepare to cope with whatever circumstances whatever person's actions may affect the future of the Principal's desired goal.

Reading the Quick Cut

Using figures 1a and 1b as examples, let's see the conclusions we can draw from them.

1. The inner card is the ten of diamonds (happiness). This immediately indicates that the attainment of the Principal's goal, or granting of his or her wish, is favorable.
2. The outer card is the seven of clubs (worries).

One way to look at the pair is that the goal's attainment will gain happiness, even if clouded by doubt or worries.

Reading the cards in the reverse order suggests that the Principal's worries will be alleviated upon the attainment of the goal, which will bring happiness to the person.

Both interpretations are in harmony, thus confirming the reading's interpretation.

First Steps in Card Reading: Exercises Using the Quick Cut

Now, what if the cards' interpretations are ambiguous or actually conflict with each other?

Let's do some exercises and cut a deck of playing cards several times and see what various interpretations you can come up with.

Use paper and a pencil or pen to jot down your notes as we go through the process. Also, this is a good time to use the Quick Card Suit Reference Table at the end of this book to help you interpret the individual cards' meanings.

You may find it interesting to compare your notes against the interpretations I derive from the following four example card cuts. I'm going to include several breaks below, between the examples, so you can stop at those points and work on your notes and interpretation before continuing with the text.

1. Inner card: eight of diamonds. Outer card: seven of hearts.

Right away we know the wish's or goal's prospect is favorable since the diamonds are a red suit. By looking at the reference table, we note that this card dually represents personal interest as well as friendly surroundings.

Remember that the seven of hearts belongs in Masha's major cards group since it stands for strong emotions, namely, jealousy.

Now, take a few minutes and see what links or connections you come up with between these two cards.

(Five minutes later . . .)

How did you do? Let's see how your conclusions compare with mine.

Since the inner card indicates there's no doubt that the goal's or wish's prospects are favorable, I examined both cards and discovered several layers for interpreting their forecast and identifying how, or under what circumstances, the goal or wish will be achieved.

Looking at the inner card, the eight of diamonds represents socializing, as well as pleasant talk. This clearly indicates that the goal will be achieved by good interaction with other people.

Further, it could also mean that through a social gathering, be it a friend's party or a business party, the Principal will find the means of attaining his or her goal or wish through new or longtime personal acquaintances.

The eight of diamonds card also implies that through polite, or friendly, discussions, the Principal may discover the means or connections to attain his or her goal or wish, be it with an individual or a group of people.

Now let's examine the outer card.

The seven of hearts identifies that jealousy is linked with the goal, so the Principal is cautioned against evoking the emotion in another person, or even within himself.

If jealousy is the emotion that spurs the Principal toward his goal or inspires his wish, the Reader ought to advise the Principal to control his sentiment and not allow it to govern his words or deeds.

Another interpretation of the same card could be that once the goal is attained, or the wish granted, the Principal ought to be discreet and not flaunt his success. Such action will most assuredly stir jealousy among his acquaintances or friends.

Together, the two cards advise the Principal to be discreet within friendly surroundings and prevent jealousy from marring the goal's attainment or wish fulfillment.

Here are three more Quick Cuts; see how you can interpret them and compare your findings with mine.

2. Inner card: seven of clubs. Outer card: eight of clubs.

The seven of clubs represents worries; the eight of clubs, job or business talk.

(Five minutes later . . .)

Since black indicates delayed goal attainment or wish fulfillment, the seven of clubs denotes that worries may be the impediment of such.

Also, the job, as represented by the eight of clubs, may be the impediment factor. Keep in mind that "job" doesn't necessarily mean the place of employment; it could also be a duty or task the Principal is responsible for.

As the eight of clubs also identifies business talk, this interpretation implies that discussions involving business—be they legal contract negotiations, general meetings with coworkers, or haggling prices at a flea market—could entail negative factors affecting the Principal's efforts.

Together the two cards imply that the worries or concerns connected to a job or business-related dialogue will deter the Principal's drive toward her goal or wish.

Just to be sure, I did a quick reverse reading of the cards to see if the interpretation holds together. . . .

A job, or results of business discussions, may evoke worries that will impede the Principal's efforts to attain her goal or fulfill her wish.

3. Inner card: four of hearts. Outer card: four of spades.

The four of hearts denotes a nice gathering, while the four of spades indicates that an atmosphere, or even a situation, is doubtful or that a person will be torn apart emotionally.

(Five minutes later . . .)

Combining the two cards' interpretations, this Quick Cut reading indicates that the goal will be achieved, or the wish granted, under pleasant surroundings, in spite of unfriendly forces' attempts at tearing apart the Principal's efforts or the Principal's own doubtful feelings while en route to realizing that goal or wish.

In reverse, despite the malevolent forces' efforts, or any doubts the Principal may feel, the goal will be achieved or the wish realized.

Once that happens, the Principal will find himself in a pleasant gathering or friendlier circumstances.

4. Inner card: king of spades. Outer card: six of diamonds.

The king of spades represents either a rival or a widower and the six of diamonds indicates a path or action taken.

(Five minutes later . . .)

One interpretation implies that the rival may take an active role in blocking the Principal's efforts, and the other that a widower may, wittingly or not, impede the Principal's actions. In both cases, the Principal may be required to take steps to deal with the person's consequential actions.

Now that you've taken your first steps in interpreting the playing cards, you can see how quickly one can pick up the meanings. In time you will become more at ease with the interpretations. Before you know it, you will only refer to the Quick Card Suit Reference Table from time to time.

In all Quick Cuts, interpretations of the cards' pips—the symbols for any suit on a playing card—will help determine not only the circumstances, but the magnitude of that situation's influence upon the Principal's path as she strives toward her objective.

Remember to take note of the direction the inner pips are pointing on the odd-numbered cards—particularly the cards with values of five and higher, regardless of suit. (To learn the subtleties, refer to the individual cards' interpretations as identified in chapter 2.)

It's important to include this observation as part of the layout's interpretation. With the exception of diamonds, a pip's orientation, or pointing direction, will also influence the reading of the layout.

Examples:
1. Ace of clubs upside down (its stem pointing up): reversal of fortune, or trouble at home.
2. Ace of spades upside down (its stem pointing up): great tragedy instead of death.
3. Ace of hearts upside down (its point pointing up): uneasiness at heart.

If, after the Quick Cut, the Principal wishes to go on to the next level of card reading, the Reader will proceed by picking up the two stacks of cards and reuniting them to form one complete deck.

The Reader reunites the cards by turning the inner card stack facedown and placing the outer card stack on top of it, also facedown. With this maneuver, the standard card-cutting procedure is completed.

The cards are *not* shuffled.

The Reader can now proceed to the next level.

THE SHORT READING

The Reader holds the playing card deck in one hand, facedown, and draws the first two cards from the top.

Placing the pair of cards on the table faceup, the Reader displays the two cards overlapped, like an opened ladies' fan, wide enough to distinguish and identify the cards' pips and the royals' suits.

If one card of the pair is not a queen or king of hearts (depending on the Principal's sex), the Reader continues to draw cards from the deck.

The next two cards are drawn and placed atop the first pair, again spread out like a fan. The Reader continually draws the cards, two by two, one pair after another, until the king or queen of hearts is revealed.

Once the Principal's card and its companion card are drawn, they are set aside, ensuring the two cards are arranged like an open fan in the same order they emerged from the deck.

The previously drawn cards are collected, without disturbing the order, and reunited with the remaining cards still held in hand. Their fan layouts are closed and they are placed atop the deck facedown.

Again, the deck is *not* to be reshuffled. (To do so would only disrupt the continuity of the reading and the Principal's initial influence or "aura" absorbed by the cards when they were shuffled.)

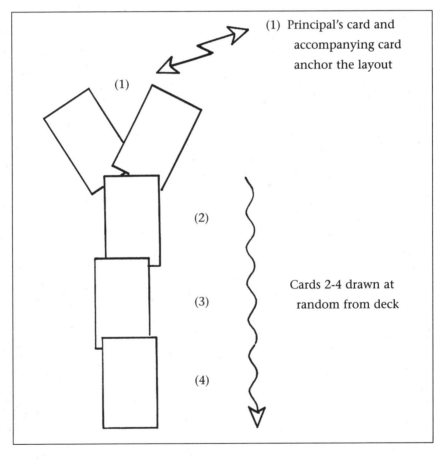

(1) Principal's card and accompanying card anchor the layout

Cards 2-4 drawn at random from deck

Figure 2. The Short Reading Layout

Once the cards are reunited to form a single deck, the Reader holds the cards and selects three cards at random from the stack. These cards are placed down, one by one and faceup, to form a cascading flow from the anchor pair, starting at their mutual base. The order in which these cards are placed down and how they should appear in the resulting layout are illustrated in figure 2.

The placement of the Principal's card, in its pairing with the accompanying card, subtly influences the meaning of its companion card, and vice versa, in the following manner:

Should the Principal's card—the queen or king of hearts—cover its companion, the latter card's influence and interpretation lies more in the area of the Principal's thoughts. There is a strong chance that the nature of that card is influencing the person's conscience, perhaps even the subconscious.

When the companion card lies on top of the Principal's queen or king of hearts, then that card's interpretation tends to deal more with a situation at hand. If nothing seems to be happening currently, there is a strong possibility that an upcoming event or situation will very soon occur in the Principal's life. This event or situation will require conscientious attention because it is upon the Principal's doorstep, so to speak, and therefore cannot be avoided.

The significance of the position of each of the next three cards drawn is in keeping with its natural influences vis-à-vis the others around it. Remember, these cards are drawn individually at random and placed down from the base of the Principal's pair as illustrated in figure 2.

If, after interpreting the five-card layout, the reading remains ambiguous to the Principal—and *only* in this case—he or she is permitted to select an extra card or two (three at most) to help clarify the reading.

Caution: Do not presume to add any optional cards just for the sake of it. Such "forcing" of an interpretation will only throw the reading into a muddle.

In other words, don't push your luck!

The Reader hands over the playing cards, still in a deck stack, to the Principal. The latter draws an extra card from anywhere in the deck and places it on whichever one of the three single cascading cards whose meaning or role he or she wishes to have further clarified.

Again, a maximum of three cards may be drawn and placed, no more. Also, a cascading card can only receive one extra card, not two, and certainly not three.

Close Observations

Watch how the Principal lays down the optional card (or cards). Does she or he place the card alongside a cascading card? Or does it touch?

The placement of the card definitely affects the interpretation of that pair, and possibly the whole layout.

Moreover, if the optional card is touching the cascading one, how does it touch? Does it cover the cascading card only on the corner or edge, halfway, or completely?

By any chance is the optional card placed crosswise to the cascading one, thus covering a large portion? Or is it so completely aligned as to cover the cascading card?

If its edge (or just its corner) touches, that optional card has some influence upon the cascading one. The influence may be minor, yet it is still direct. At halfway, the optional card's influence is more prominent.

If the optional card covers the cascading one completely (which means it also covers the next cascading card partially), then that aspect could denote an obsession or an overwhelming action (undertaken by either the Principal or another person, depending on its identity and/or role). If the card represents an object or sentiment, it could be an obstacle for the Principal or caused by the Principal.

You can see how the simple placement of a card holds subtle nuances that are important to consider.

• • •

If the Short Reading piques the Principal's curiosity, he or she may opt to go to the next (and final) level: the Detailed Reading.

From my experiences in reading the playing cards over the years, I've found that in many instances the more detailed layout can further explain what the cards in the simpler layouts are trying to tell the Principal.

THE DETAILED READING

This layout can stand on its own or be the final stage of a comprehensive set of readings.

If this reading follows the Short Reading for the same Principal, the Reader retains the queen or king of hearts and has the Principal shuffle the remaining cards three times. This reinforces the connection between the Principal and the cards.

Should this be the initial reading, the queen or king of hearts card is set aside and the deck thoroughly shuffled by the Principal until he or she feels satisfied with the process and stops.

Order of Placement

The Reader takes back the cards and holds the shuffled deck facedown in one hand in order to draw cards with the free hand. The cards are drawn from the top in consecutive order, singly at first, then in pairs.

The first card is drawn, held facedown, and slipped under and crosswise to the Principal's card. This card represents the Principal's subconscious mind and/or thoughts that influence his or her actions, philosophy, or outlook.

The next card drawn is also kept facedown and placed atop, and slightly to the right of, the Principal's card, crosswise. This card depicts the Principal's conscious mind—in effect, his or her private thoughts. Moreover, this card could explain the possible reason (or reasons) motivating the Principal's words or deeds.

The last of the single cards drawn is placed faceup this time, in a portrait position (as opposed to lying crosswise in a landscape position) to the right of the Principal's card. It should slightly overlap the third, or private thoughts, card. This exposed card represents a subject or emotion the Principal may have discussed with a close friend or, depending on the card's interpretation, with all and sundry. In all likelihood, this card has the enhanced power of influencing the Principal's conscious thought.

The rest of the cards are drawn in pairs and placed faceup and spread like fans. Be sure to safeguard the cards' overlapping order as you draw and set them down. The order reveals each card's influence upon its mate. To disregard such detail, at any level of any of the layouts, can erroneously affect the interpretation and miscast the reading.

The first pair is placed above the Principal's cards (at the twelve o'clock position), the next pair below (at six o'clock). The following two pairs are set on either side of the Principal's cards—a pair to the left of the Principal's cards at nine o'clock, and the next pair at the three o'clock position. The final four pairs are set down in clockwise order to fill the remaining spaces, starting at the gap between the twelve and three o'clock positions. The last pair of cards drawn and set down close the layout and cocoon the Principal's card.

The resulting detailed card layout is illustrated in figure 3. You will note that the playing cards in the figure are numbered to illustrate the order in which they are to be set down, singly at first, then in pairs.

With time and practice, the Reader will soon be able to capture a "snapshot impression" of the cards' interpretation, and get a preview, so to speak, on whether the reading will be favorable or not. A Reader can absorb some immediate clues, for example, from the predominant color in the layout, the ratio of royals to numbered cards, and the suits represented.

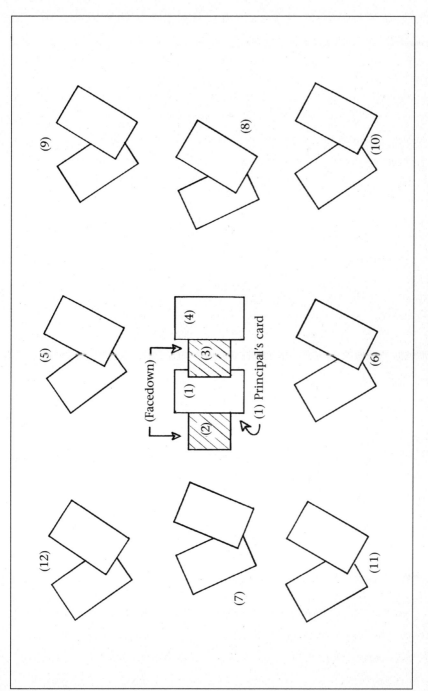

Figure 3. The Detailed Reading Layout
(Numbers denote sequence order of cards drawn.)

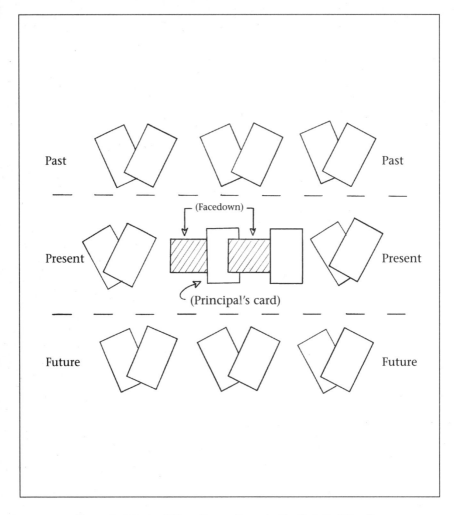

Figure 4. Principal Time Frame Rows in the Detailed Reading

Rows, Columns, and Bubbles

The Detailed Reading's layout comprises columns and rows, like a tic-tac-toe board, with two "bubbles" located in the lowest row. One of these bubbles is a pair of cards in the left-hand corner, and the other encompasses both the center pair and the pair in the right-hand corner.

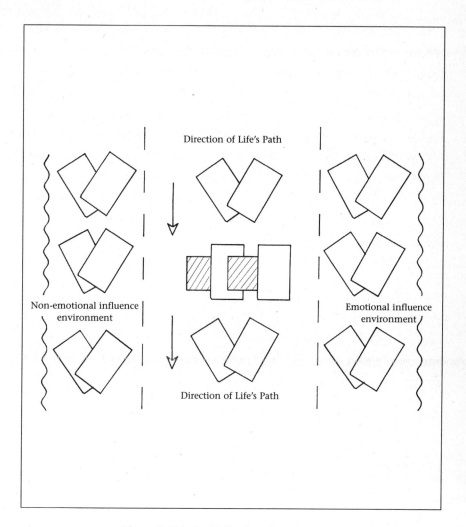

Figure 5. Principal's Path and Environment

Let's start by learning the layout's column row sections, shown in figure 4.

The middle row, containing the Principal's card cluster, is seen as representing present-day circumstances and/or surroundings. As the Principal's card is considered to be facing the future, the row above the queen or king of hearts depicts the past, which could be recent or some time ago. The lower row is regarded as the immediate future, which on the average encompasses time from as soon as the next few hours following the reading up to roughly four weeks into the future.

Let's now look at the layout's column sections, shown in figure 5.

The two outer columns represent the Principal's environment, and the middle column is the path the Principal travels upon through life. Consider that the queen or king's progress is forward—or in the downward direction in the layout. Thus, the bottom area shows the future the Principal will encounter upon the path he or she is taking, and the upper portion of the column shows what has already happened on the Principal's path.

In figure 5, arrows signify the Principal's path and direction of travel.

The cards in the column to the right of the Principal's card depict matters close to the heart. These cards may signify the emotional connection and/or influence of people or circumstances between them and the Principal, like loving family support, or worries at work, or anticipation of an event. Thus, overall, the meaning of the cards lying in that column would be of interest to the Principal from an emotional viewpoint.

The cards in the column to the left of the Principal are just as important, but depict the nonemotional environmental influences.

Earlier, I mentioned the "bubbles" that encompass certain cards. The positions of the bubbles are illustrated in figure 6.

These areas are worthy to note, as they may play significant parts in the Principal's possible future or interests. In the case of the larger bubble, which encompasses four future cards, its collective interpretation may also evoke considerable emotional influence. Note that this bubble lies on the emotional side of the Principal's card.

The smaller bubble, encompassing one pair of cards in the lower left-hand corner, depicts an element in the Principal's future. Its influence is so negligible that it could be regarded as something just in passing. One may almost regard this as a minor event, affecting the

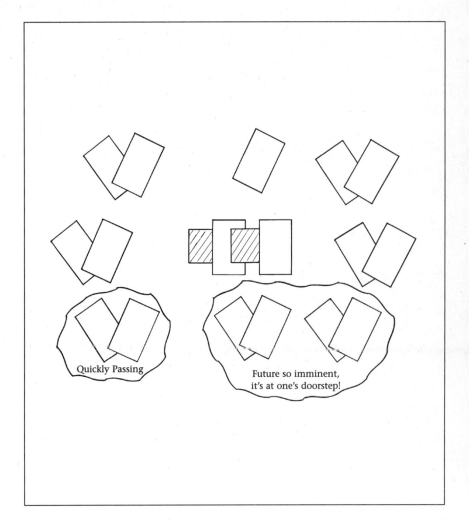

Figure 6. Future "Bubbles"

environment more than directly affecting the Principal, but do not dismiss the event completely. These two cards still have something to say!

The larger bubble includes the pairs of cards lying at the center and lower right-hand corner of the future's row. This grouping of cards signals an element so immediate in proximity to the Principal that it could be (figuratively) stepped on! These important cards can help the Principal to become aware of, and possibly prepare for, an upcoming situation or event. One such event, for example, may be an encounter the Principal will have with a person or persons (when royal cards are present) that would be of great interest to all the parties concerned.

Moreover, I've seen these particular cards, on more than one occasion, serve as a timely "heads up!" warning. I'm glad to report, from past readings, that the Principals who have received such warnings and heeded them were able to become prepared (even emotionally so). They were able to encounter their particular situations without being caught off guard.

Order of Interpretation

My preferred order of interpreting the Detailed Reading's layout is to start with the past, go through the present, and proceed to the future.

Then I conclude the first run-through by discussing each of the center cards, or the Principal's connecting cards, starting with the exposed card (on the right, number four in order of drawing and setting down on the layout).

This outer card I call the Public Knowledge card. It represents a thought or idea the Principal may have discussed with a close friend or perhaps a general topic he or she may have talked about with friends at large.

Next I turn over the card resting facedown crosswise between the Principal's card and the Public Knowledge card. I refer to this card as the Principal's Private Thoughts.

The last card I reveal is the remaining facedown crosswise card, the one beneath the Principal's card. This one I call the Subconscious Mind card. This card can be quite important and I prefer to leave it for interpretation last, for I regard it as the "key" to the Principal's actions.

This last card could represent an event in the Principal's past that, though it may have been forgotten, has impressed the Principal so much as to subtly influence his or her thoughts and/or actions.

Once I have interpreted this last card, I reexamine the Private Thoughts and Public Knowledge cards and review the Detail Reading's layout once more. The Subconscious Mind card, many times in conjunction with the Private Thoughts card, may reveal the key factor to interpreting the Principal's card layout.

There are many people whose everyday actions or long-term plans are influenced by an episode in their lives from long ago, sometimes as far back as their childhood.

Such experiences can often be the cornerstone of good.

For example, the self-made person's childhood of poverty and deprivation may have been the impetus to make something of him- or herself and become a philanthropist.

Or a medical science researcher may work tirelessly on finding cures for terminal diseases because he or she lost someone close and was compelled to find a way to help others avoid such tragic fates.

Also keep in mind that there is a flip side to this coin.

Terrible experiences in the past could scar some people and make them lash out at others for the rest of their sad lives.

Consider the Subconscious Mind card carefully before you voice anything.

I usually wait till I've examined the layout completely and worked out the interrelationships of the cards before informing the Principal of the reading's interpretation.

There will be times when the layout is a joy to relate to the Principal. And there will be times when discretion *is* the better part of valor.

Within the pages of this book you will encounter one or two cases I read where the cards were quite disturbing, and have placed one or two people on the defensive side.

Take note, however—they have not denied the truth of the cards!

FOREWARNED IS FOREARMED

Below are two short narratives, with the more intimate details omitted, as both ladies are my friends. Both are very much in the public eye, and one is even regarded as a local celebrity.

What I describe is general public knowledge because they have discussed and described some aspects of their experiences. Yet very few outside these ladies' circle of intimates are aware that they had card readings done by me, and that the forecast experiences that came to pass were "all in the cards."

Ms. A

On one occasion I gave card readings during a cozy gathering of Ms. A's close friends. In one reading, to the surprise and bafflement of all present, including the Principal (Ms. A), the cards' prediction was rather gloomy.

The layout forecast a split between two people, heartbreak, and turmoil. However, while the warning cards lay in the future row, the royals surrounding the Principal's queen of hearts in the remaining areas of the detailed layout clearly suggested the presence of a strong network of friends and support that would see her through the upcoming serious event.

As much as the Principal and her friends speculated, no one could even begin to guess what could happen that would fit this scenario. Well, as intriguing as the reading was, the ladies' curiosity soon tapered off as time passed while they all went on with their busy lives. Even I forgot about it until I ran into Ms. A sometime later, shortly after her return from one of her many overseas speaking engagements.

As it turned out, the hardworking, gentle, and beloved lady's life had taken an unexpected turn shortly after that afternoon's party. Her long-lived marriage had suddenly dissolved when her husband, out of the blue, decided to leave her.

Even today, she expresses how she is still impressed that the reading fulfilled its prediction and by how accurate it was. Ms. A confirms that all through the divorce proceedings, her friends and family rallied around her. Their steadfast love and support helped her come through what was one of the most stressful periods of her life.

Ms. B

Another reading that impressed a Principal was Ms. B's; her reading predicted health concerns for a close relation and that financial matters would be involved.

Being a good friend of Ms. A, Ms. B was well aware of the cards' accuracy in their forecasts and in their ability to confirm disclosures of a Principal's present and past circumstances. She was therefore receptive to the cautionary note her reading carried.

Within a couple of weeks, the Principal's mother suffered an accident in a public place and the injury resulting from the incident was serious enough to raise legal action.

Now, be reassured that not all predictions are negative.

The two readings were cited in order to serve as examples of how a Principal can be alerted to upcoming events. And, thanks to the cards, he or she can be more or less prepared for any such events, especially if the prediction made is unfavorable.

Forewarned is forearmed. . . .

PRACTICE MAKES PERFECT (OR NEARLY SO!)

Now that you've read through the descriptions of the Quick Cut, the Short Reading, and the Detailed Reading, it's time to start practicing and become more familiar with the procedure.

You've tried your first steps with the Quick Cut reading and you've discovered how easy it is to do. It's also so nice and straightforward that you can easily create your own exercises. Just take a few minutes with a standard deck of playing cards. Cut the deck and read the inner and outer cards. With each additional practice session you assign yourself, I have all confidence in you that you'll pick up the Quick Cut's interpretive method in no time at all.

The challenge for you, dear apprentice Reader, will lie in learning the other two layouts: the Short Reading and the Detailed Reading.

In chapter 5, you'll be provided with several interpretation exercises for both higher levels, using the readings I've done in the past and recorded. These are also samplings of the many readings that have proven themselves.

Try your hand at interpreting them before you read my explanations of what was predicted and what actually happened.

Take your time, especially when you tackle the interpretation of the Detailed Readings, which definitely become more multilayered once you start dealing with the interrelationships among the cards. Remember, the Quick Card Suit Reference Table will be a handy tool for you!

Sample Readings

*A*mong *Sergei's sketches, which Katya inherited after* his death, many were without any annotations about the outcome of those readings. So it is not known if the predictions were ever fulfilled or not. Yet several of them are so interesting that I decided to include them in this book as helpful examples of card reading in general.

I recommend to a beginner Reader, while you are learning the individual meanings of the cards, that you lay out each of the seven-card readings as listed below, then try to interpret the layout in your own way. Maybe even jot down your own interpretations on a piece of paper. After you've done that, compare your reading with Masha's and see how accurate you are. You will find Masha's interpretations starting on page 79.

Keep in mind that card reading is not an exact science. No need to be disappointed if your reading slightly differs from Masha's. There is no monopoly on fortune telling, especially not card reading. Think of how different the horoscopes in two different publications can be. Remember, interpretation can be expressed differently, as long as the overall meaning is the same.

But if your reading is completely different, and you have mistaken a wedding for a funeral, an argument for a pleasant talk, or happiness for a big sorrow, then return the cards into the deck. Shuffle, and start working on the next sample. Wait at least a day or two before you return to the same exercise.

Don't make the mistake of trying to memorize any of the layouts. Instead, concentrate on remembering what the individual cards stand for.

Do the same exercise with the Short Reading and the Detailed Reading layouts given in chapter 5, and before you know it, you'll be an "expert."

Then you can try to do a Detailed Reading for yourself or for someone very close to you. This way you will be more relaxed; also, knowing your own life, you'll be able to compare the layout to what you know of your own situation, and see if they concur. You will also have more time to concentrate on what you see.

Once you gain confidence in your ability, offer to read the cards to a relative or a good friend who will not criticize or laugh at you if you are inconsistent in your interpretations. Explain to them that you are a novice and ask them for their patience. You will be surprised how cooperative people can be. And, before you know it, by looking at the cards, the words will start coming out of your mouth automatically as if your intuition, not your intellect, is governing what you say.

You will not only be reading the cards, you will be interpreting them. You will be able to absorb the existent vibes in the air. Don't think you'll feel some breeze or electric shock. You won't start trembling or go into a trance. Nothing like that. But there is something unexplainable that happens between the Reader, the cards, and the Principal. Most importantly, you have to relax completely. A tense person can never be a good Reader.

There is also no guarantee that you will ever become an exceptional fortune teller. Yet, who knows? With practice and patience . . . as I said before, you are on your own.

Okay. Let's start practicing.

For identification purposes with the exercises, I will use the same code system that Sergei used nearly two hundred years ago on his sketches.

When he made a sketch of Masha's cards, he would mark them with the date and initials of the person involved. Later, when the results of that particular reading became public, he would add them in detail to the sketch.

So when you lay out the cards under the entry "L.B. March 1824," look for the answers on page 81 under the same code.

To re-create Masha's layouts the first two cards are paired and set down side by side and the rest are cascaded below the pair in a single column.

SAMPLES OF MASHA'S SEVEN-CARD LAYOUTS

Keep in mind that the patrons of the establishment where Masha sang didn't go there for card readings. Occasionally somebody would ask for one, mostly in jest. Then, Masha would use her seven-card method, with great success.

It was short and straight to the point and satisfied the customer. As they all were men, the "Principal" card in those exercises was always the king of hearts. If you substitute the king with the queen of hearts, you will realize that the same readings dealing with love, health, money, and other of life's problems can easily be applied to the lifestyle of a modern woman. So if for any reason you prefer using a queen of hearts in your exercises, go ahead.

1. L.B. March 1824
   king of hearts to ace of diamonds
   nine of clubs
   four of diamonds
   six of diamonds
   knight of clubs
   nine of diamonds

My educated guess would be that you have (with the help of the reference table) properly identified the cards. Now read those cards and write down your interpretation, and see how it compares with Masha's.

2. Y.C. December 1824.
   After comparing your reading with Masha's you will realize why I have chosen this as the next exercise.

   king of hearts to nine of spades
   knight of spades
   seven of clubs
   six of hearts
   king of clubs
   ten of diamonds

3. K.K. May 1825
   king of hearts to two of diamonds
   eight of spades
   queen of clubs
   two of spades
   four of spades
   ace of hearts

4. B.W. April 1828
   There is no story about this reading, only two annotations of later dates in the lower right-hand corner of the sketch. I assume they have something to do with the prophesy.

   king of hearts to ace of diamonds
   seven of hearts
   king of spades
   queen of hearts
   eight of hearts
   three of diamonds

   May 1828
   October 1828

5. A.K. May 1830
   king of hearts to three of hearts
   five of clubs
   knight of clubs
   three of clubs
   nine of hearts
   ten of clubs

6. D.H. May 1830
   king of hearts to three of diamonds
   ten of clubs
   nine of clubs
   ace of hearts
   queen of hearts
   nine of hearts

Masha's Interpretations of the Seven-Card Layouts

Following are Masha's comments on the preceding layouts, also taken from Sergei's sketches. Keep in mind that he wrote in Russian. I did my best to translate them as literally as possible.

When you compare her interpretations with your readings, think twice before you come to any conclusions. If you have read the cards accurately you will notice a similarity in the overall meaning of the reading.

1. L.B. March 1824
   You will receive an official letter, which will require your decision about certain steps—measures to be taken. But before you decide what to do, you should consult a friend who could give you advice.

2. Y.C. December 1824
   A health problem is causing you serious worries. A trip to a doctor's office will dissipate your fears and you will be very happy again. Your health will improve.

3. K.K. May 1825

Your meeting with an older female relative (it could be your mother, your aunt, or even your godmother) will result in a terrible argument that will leave you with a heavy heart. You know you are right, but you'll suffer out of love and respect for that woman.

4. B.W. April 1828

You will receive news that will consume you with jealousy because of a rival standing between you and your romantic interest. Don't worry. The lady is only flirting. In the end you will succeed in winning her affection.

5. A.K. May 1830

You are to achieve a very personal success through hard work and perseverance. You will gain friendship, respect, and riches.

6. D.H. May 1830

All your wishes will be granted. You gain financially through a successful business and your heart's desire will be fulfilled by the woman you love.

RARE AND INTERESTING LAYOUTS

The following is an exceptionally rare reading. It occurred more than eighty years ago, and the whole episode was faithfully recorded by one of the participants.

The year is 1916. The country is at war, the czar is in trouble, the political situation is unstable. An intimate group of friends unite at Zina's (now Countess Zinaida Petrovna) for dinner.

It is the eve of the year 1917. After dinner, the group is engaged in the ancient custom of dropping a spoonful of melted wax into cold water, then holding the cluster of hardened wax between a candle flame and the wall. The shadow the piece of wax casts shows what awaits the person in the next year. Needless to say, there is always lots of laughter over this parlor game, as it is hard to agree on what the shadow represents.

Among those present is Zina's mother, Tasha. Retired from her Gypsy life of song, dance, and fortune telling, she now reads the cards exclusively to close friends.

Asked to do so now, not to anybody personally, but for the new year, she said, "Fine. The first card I lay on the table shall be the 'Principal' event of the coming year."

That first card was the ten of spades. By the time she put the last card down on the table, the layout consisted of only royals and spades. Deadly silence reigned in the room. Tasha was speechless. After looking at the cards for a long time, she crossed herself.

"Devil's work! I have never seen cards like this. Complete devastation. Death. Tears. Nobody is spared. Men, women, children. I don't know what to say."

She didn't have to say anything. History said it all.

By the end of the next year, 1917, Russia was in turmoil. Revolution swept the country. The assassination of the czar and his family shocked the world. Mayhem was everywhere. By the end of the year, of all present on that New Years Eve, only Zina was still alive.

Until the end of her days, Zina was able to visualize that terrible layout and describe it to my mother, who in turn recorded it in her notebook. Mother reluctantly gave me permission to include information about it in this book.

It is a terrible layout, but it's so rare, I just had to use it as a sample.

PERSONAL LESSONS IN READING THE CARDS

Once in a while, the larger bubble of cards dominates the lower center and lower right-hand corner of the Detailed Reading's layout, in the position that represents a future so imminent, it is almost at one's doorstep.

The following samples should give you an idea.

Just for fun, my neighbor's husband asked me for a reading. He flatly stated he didn't believe in "those things" but was curious to see what it was all about. As he was embarrassed to visit a psychic, and knowing that I do read for friends, he asked me if I would do it for him. The cards on his doorstep were the king of clubs and ace of clubs, the ten of clubs and six of clubs.

"The visit of an older man is going to bring you a large sum of money, but you'll have to take a trip."

The poor man, who had a large family, was struggling to make ends meet. He laughed at my prediction. "Sure! I'll win ten million dollars and they are going to deliver it to my doorstep."

His comment made me laugh long after he left, after thanking me for the experience.

Several weeks later a basket of fruits was delivered, with a note to me. "Thank you! John."

When I scolded him for the unnecessary expense, he said, "Don't worry, I'm a rich man." And then he explained that a real estate agent had approached him with a more than generous offer for his house. The client who wanted to buy it was born in that house and now wanted to spend his retirement years living there. The money he offered was enough for John to buy another home and have some left over to put into the bank.

I have a feeling I made him respect card reading, if not believe in it.

Occasionally, a layout is interpreted as very hard to handle, as it was for me in the next case.

A couple of years back, I read the cards to an acquaintance of mine. In the lower right-hand corner of the Detailed Reading's layout were the knight of hearts (child) and the nine of spades (funeral). In the lower center, the seven of spades (tears) and the six of spades (failure). I was speechless. How could I tell the mother that on her doorstep lurked the death of her only child?

After taking a closer look at the rest of the layout, I was even more astounded.

The cards indicated nothing but happiness and joy. The ten of diamonds, the ten of hearts, the nine of hearts, and the five of hearts mingled with other friendly cards.

Impossible. How could the death of a little boy bring so much joy to his mother?

I could not continue the reading, so I hastily, in a few words, told the woman the pleasant things in the layout and dispatched her with the warning to watch her child.

I was very dissatisfied with that reading. For weeks, that layout would pop up in my thoughts and I would try to figure out how could I best tell her the truth.

Then it happened. I read it in the newspapers. The woman's son and his friend were riding their bicycles on the sidewalk in front of her house when a speeding car plowed into them. The woman's son was thrown from his bike unhurt, but the other little boy was killed instantly.

Now I understood. The tears were for the little boy who died in front of her home, and the joy and happiness were because her son survived the accident.

When I was in college, my roommate asked me to read the cards to her mother, who was visiting. Her mother had brought a friend with her, so I read the cards to both women.

The friend of the mother had the seven of spades and the five of spades in the upper left-hand corner, and the upper center was covered with the knight of hearts and the three of spades.

"Some time ago," I said to her, "you shed lots of tears because of the loss of a child."

"I was never married," the woman replied, somewhat tartly.

Because my roommate and her mother were present I didn't go into further explanations but finished the reading. The woman was satisfied and even left "pizza" money for me and my roommate.

That evening, when we were alone, my roommate told me that rumor had it that the woman, when in her teens, had had a baby, whom she'd given up for adoption.

I hate it when an unpleasant past shows up in the layout. It is usually something kept secret by the Principal. If the Principal denies something that's in the cards, you are obliged to change the subject and continue the reading of the other cards in the layout.

A man came to me once, who worked on a nearby construction project. His sister, one of my neighbors, sent him. I really didn't see why, but as a favor to my neighbor I read him the cards.

The entire upper row of his Detail Reading's layout consisted of the four of spades, the seven of clubs, the knight of spades, the three of clubs, the three of diamonds, and the seven of diamonds.

It was clear he was torn apart and worried about some past trouble that was causing an obstacle for the success of his plans.

Sure enough, he confessed that, because of a drunken hit-and-run accident a few years back, he'd spent some time in prison. He was a teacher, but because of the police record he lost his right to teach and the only job he could find was as a carpenter.

So be careful when you are doing readings and be sensitive to the Principal's past, and his or her privacy, and be gentle about revealing negative or troublesome information.

More Exercises

*B*efore doing the following exercises, I encourage you to review chapter 3, especially the sections covering the Detailed Layout's finer points and nuances of interpretation. Also refer to the Quick Card Suit Reference Table frequently to help you decipher the initial meaning of the card.

Refer to chapter 2 as well, constantly if necessary, for an individual card's detailed meaning and how its interpretation is affected by certain accompanying cards, because they could play important roles in the reading.

With each exercise, I'll first provide a little background and what prompted the Principal to approach me for a reading. Included may be the thoughts or feelings he or she shared with me before we started the session or while he or she shuffled the cards.

Regarding the Short Reading, I selected the layouts in which the Principal elected to draw all three optional cards. Remember, in addition to how those cards are set down along the cascading cards, their influence is also defined by how they are positioned: alongside, touching, on top of, or across a cascading row card. If an optional card is placed atop a cascading one, note how it's placed—how much of the cascading card does it obscure?

To develop your skill, each ensuing exercise gradually increases in complexity.

For your information, any of the Principal's private thoughts, previously unmentioned, were shared with me after the reading, or when the prediction came true. You will soon discover that a Principal will volunteer the reason they asked for the reading, even if you don't ask.

Like my predecessors, I've made it a custom to note the more interesting readings. This now makes it possible for me to share them with you for instructional purposes.

Each interpretation exercise is accompanied by a drawing. Examine each picture to see how the cards are positioned, copy the layout identically using your own deck of cards and interpret what you see.

Give yourself about fifteen minutes for practice at the start, no more, so as not to burn yourself out during your apprenticeship to card interpretation! I'll indicate where in each exercise you should pause for fifteen minutes to study the cards and interpret the layout. Following these breaks I'll give my own interpretations. See how close your interpretations are to mine. No doubt you'll be surprised at how well you do!

Finally, practice, practice, practice. After going through these exercises, give yourself a day or two off before you do them again. Do them in order of complexity or, just as a personal challenge, choose exercises at random.

Then, it's time to move on to reading for yourself. Remember, you'll gain confidence much more quickly by working alone and interpreting your own layouts to start with. Before long you'll quickly recognize each card's meaning and soon find yourself reading your friends' fortunes!

SHORT READING EXERCISES

These examples of readings I have done will give you an opportunity to practice your card reading skills.

Exercise 1—Worried Manager

A friend of mine was quite disturbed with the atmosphere at his place of employment and asked me to read his fortune.

Though his job was secure enough, he felt that he was in limbo owing to project freezes. Moreover, the fact that the company was making news headlines with speculations that it was on the brink of a shakeout only added fuel to the staff rumor mill. It was understandable that Mr. F, along with everyone else, was concerned about job security.

We privately met in his office and I laid out the cards. As I expected, he elected to go ahead and draw all three optional cards. His Short Reading is illustrated here.

(Fifteen minutes later . . .)

Right away I could see how strongly the cards had "absorbed" his concerns.

The six of diamonds tucked in behind the Principal's card clearly confirmed his mental activity. Moreover, the next two cards (five of clubs and knight of diamonds) confirmed the stasis state of affairs he was experiencing at the office. The five of clubs showed that his expectations were at a standstill—they weren't materializing nor were they floundering.

The next pair of cards (four of diamonds and three of clubs) alerted him

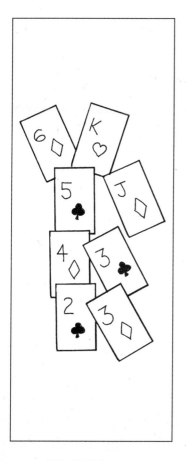

Worried Manager

that he was approaching a crossroads point in his life and that a decision would require diligence.

The final two cards (two of clubs and three of diamonds) confirmed that the efforts he was investing in his new path would lead him to a business meeting that would bring about the goal he sought.

At the end of the reading, the Principal confirmed that he would be undertaking some financial decisions very soon, and he found the reading encouraging. Two weeks later Mr. F made his decision and accepted a well-placed position in a government administration office in a major city.

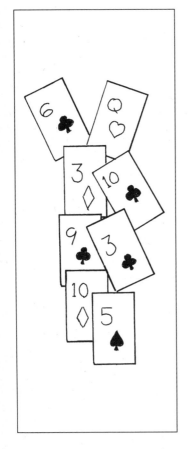

Businesswoman

Exercise 2—Businesswoman

At the start of a new year, a young career woman asked to have her cards read. Dynamic Ms. C was an excellent manager and had steadily risen from the ranks through dedication and hard work.

The Fortune 500 company she worked for was her first permanent employer (she had previously been a consultant). Ms. C not only felt an allegiance, she felt she had an obligation to repay her bosses' vote of confidence in her to do the job.

She put in a lot of hours and was rewarded often with praise, promotions, and bonuses.

Ms. C wanted to have her fortune told "just for fun" and out of curiosity. As she was in her usual state of rush between appointments, she only had time for the Short Reading.

(Fifteen minutes later . . .)

The cards easily reflected Ms. C's total commitment to her job. They foretold how her career path would gain her monetary satisfaction. Then came the warning flag in the middle and lowest pairs of cards.

They indicated the concentration and hard work she'd devote to her work. Unfortunately, her happiness would suffer.

As it turned out, she was promoted to a coveted vice presidency, but from that point on, the new responsibilities this position entailed consumed any free time she had.

Her personal life started to suffer. As a single mother she felt guilty that her baby saw more of the nanny than of her, so to make up for it, she gave up whatever little social life she had left.

Exercise 3—Anxious Young Man

An anxious young man, struggling with embarrassment, asked me if I would read his fortune. Mr. L explained that for some time he had been wooing a female coworker. Happily, she appeared to be quite receptive to his attention.

In fact, she was always delighted to go out with him and she was definitely more than friendly toward him. Mr. L knew that he was the only man she dated, and he was proud to have such an attractive young lady at his side.

Now, Mr. L confided, he felt ready to go to the next level of their relationship. He had even saved enough money for an engagement ring. Yet, he hesitated in popping the question, because she was such a beauty. There were plenty of other men who paid attention to her, and she was quite friendly toward them.

To top it off, while Mr. L and she exchanged kisses and cuddles, they never declared their love for each other. He felt somewhat unsure of her reception to his proposal of marriage and hoped the cards might indicate his prospects.

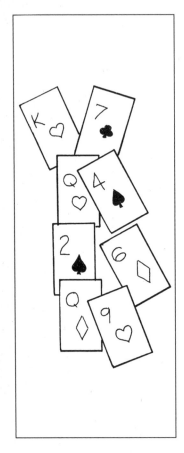

Anxious Young Man

(Fifteen minutes later . . .)

The cards had absorbed his feelings thoroughly. His worries were confirmed and they noted his doubts regarding his love interest. The cards forecast a parting of the ways and implied that in doing so he would go on with his life. In time he would find love either by meeting a young lady or through contact with a woman who was like a mother to him.

As it turned out, his love interest had been playing him along. She'd been blithely accepting his attention, gifts, and meals while she awaited her foreign boyfriend's visit during a break from his overseas assignment.

It was a foregone conclusion that the Principal would split up with her when he discovered the truth.

I'm pleased to report that he did meet another young lady, and, after several years of marriage, they're happily awaiting the birth of their second child.

The next reading is connected with the case in exercise 3. It interested me particularly for the sheer coincidence that the young man's love interest also approached me for a reading.

At the time I read her cards, his layout's prediction hadn't yet come true.

Exercise 4—Curious Young Woman

Bubbly Ms. R (Mr. L's original love interest from exercise 3) came to me within days of Mr. L's meeting with me.

Intrigued to see if a connection would reveal itself in the cards, I agreed, wisely refraining from mentioning that I had read her boyfriend's cards a few days earlier.

Though she was interested in her future in general, she was frankly interested to find out if any predictions about her love life would show up.

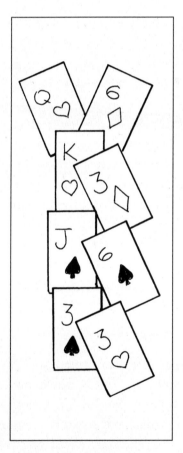

Curious Young Woman

Ms. R admitted to having a sweet-heart, but she was overwhelmed by the attentions paid to her by other bachelors at work.

(Fifteen minutes later . . .)

The cards plainly showed her thoughts were with her love interest—and that she was to get her wish through him. However, trouble lay ahead through unwise action. The warning finished with the last two cards (three of spades and three of hearts) in that they predicted she would suffer a separation or be cut off from someone (or something) that only she, apparently, would be responsible for.

Only time clarified this reading.

Yes, she was thinking of her boyfriend—the foreign one, that is. She did marry the foreigner, thereby getting her wish. (He earned a much higher salary than Mr. L did, and could afford to give her the life she wanted.)

However, over the course of two years, their marriage stagnated, their lives grew apart, and trouble developed. Then she discovered he had been using her from the start. She quickly got a divorce but he still got his green card.

The cards' prediction that her bad decisions, regarding both men, would cause her to lose out came true.

Exercise 5—Commuter Buddy

Commuter Buddy

On an Amtrak train ride home one Friday, I offered a commuter buddy a reading instead of playing our usual gin rummy game. He was tickled by the idea and readily agreed.

Mr. T, an easygoing fellow and all-around nice guy, had a good home life and business career. He numbered as one of the fortunate few who had no major concerns dominating his thoughts.

In such a relaxed state of mind, the cards were receptive to his good vibrations and nicely reflected his gregarious personality.

(Fifteen minutes later . . .)

The cards easily confirmed Mr. T's friendly demeanor and sociable personality as well as that he was a hardworking individual and regarded home life important. The only cloud on his horizon, so to speak, was trouble connected with a friendship. A rift was predicted in the future for him, between himself and a young man.

The last two pairs of cards definitely made my friend frown in puzzlement. He couldn't imagine anyone he'd part company with, let alone have trouble with. He got along with everyone and, as far as he was aware, everyone liked him.

I remember asking him whether he had a friend he'd lost touch with. He thought about it and his brow cleared. There was someone he hadn't heard from in a while, and if I hadn't asked that question, he wouldn't have realized that it'd been weeks rather than just days since they'd last spoken.

On the following Monday we met on the train again and Mr. T reported that he'd been able to hear news of his young friend. A career military man, his friend had been shipped out on short notice for active duty during a military crisis overseas. When that friend would return home was anyone's guess.

This rift shown by the cards is also an example of separation that can be caused by distance rather than any disagreement or problem.

DETAILED READING EXERCISES

These examples of readings I have done will give you practice developing your skills at the more complicated Detailed Reading.

Exercise 6—Widow's Fate

A lovely widow in her late thirties was encouraged by her girlfriend to meet me and have a reading done. Ms. W had hesitated at first but finally agreed to accompany her friend to have tea at my home. My first impression of her when we were introduced was that she was a very nice person, yet quiet and somewhat melancholy.

When the time came for Ms. W's reading, she shuffled the cards and told me that she had no particular wish or desire to express. I reassured her that that was okay and that she could just relax and let her thoughts drift. The cards would be able to reveal her future more freely with a clear mind.

And that they did. The cards' layout plainly revealed her sad past.

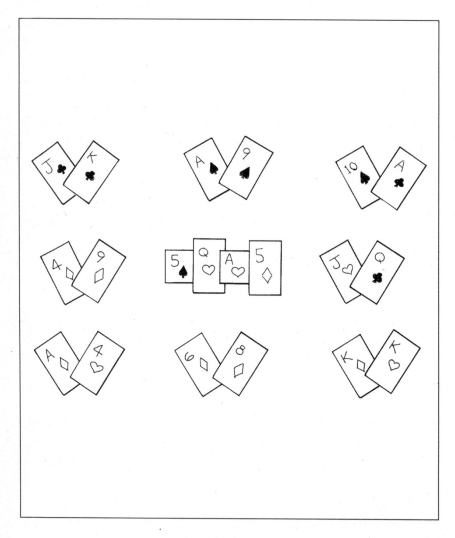

Widow's Fate

(Fifteen minutes later . . .)

The woman did have a tragic past; she had lost her husband a few years prior to my reading. Ms. W still felt his absence keenly. The cards showed how her friends and family rallied around her during her mourning and gave her moral support.

Her Principal card's neighboring cards showed that though her loss still affected her, her heart was open and giving. She readily offered friendship.

The nine and four of diamonds seemed to indicate the widow was surrounded with a friendly atmosphere. The queen of clubs alluded to a close lady friend who seemed to have hope, possibly that the Principal would finally come out of her mourning.

The cards went on to foretell how Ms. W would get an invitation to a nice gathering and predicted that she would make the effort to socialize. In doing so, the Principal will possibly meet a young man and perhaps gain a love interest either with him or through him.

The cards were right.

Ms. W did meet a very nice young man, who became greatly attracted to her. Though she's not remarried—yet—she has been seeing him steadily. I'm pleased to say that, as of this writing, their relationship is developing quite nicely and I expect the best results.

Exercise 7—Ambitious Executive

An overachiever marched up to me one day and declared that he wanted a detailed reading.

Mr. E was a young executive "on the move," as he boasted, speeding along the corporate fast track, you see, and having a great time with his success. He just had to know what lay before him and decided to come to me when he found out about my card reading skill.

Mr. E laughingly confessed to me that he didn't believe in stuff like psychics, horoscopes, palm readers, and such, but for a lark he wanted to have his cards read and fortune told anyway. He decided to

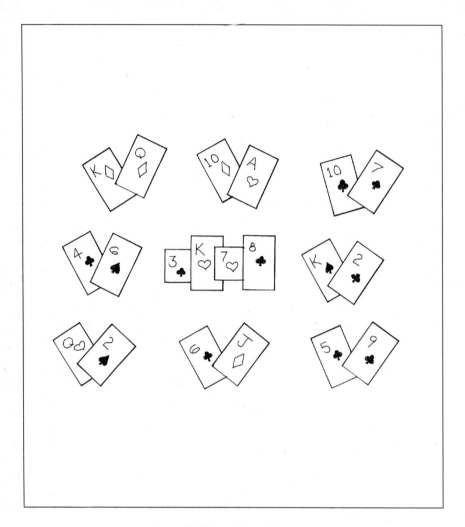

Ambitious Executive

simply regard the Detailed Reading as his "corporate fuzz buster" and see if there were any back stabbers lurking in his future.

(Fifteen minutes later . . .)

The cards showed him to have a good past, filled with friends and happiness, even though there were worries connected with money matters.

The cards depicting his present circumstances focused on his rapidly advancing career. They were correct in disclosing that Mr. E's work consumed his thoughts and actions, which were more than likely motivated by jealousy. He was also experiencing (if not already, then very soon) financial insecurity in connection with some unwise action.

In addition to confirming his present state of affairs, the cards predicted he would encounter a rival, or rivalry, at a business meeting, or find out about such through a business meeting. This encounter would have an emotional impact on him.

The cards continued to foretell that he would embark on a business trip with expectations. However, he would not only suffer a loss through that enterprise but he would experience a rift between himself and his love interest.

The cards were clear in their cautionary warning that he not carry false hopes, and, further, that he not neglect his sweetheart or alienate her affection as a result of his work drive.

The young executive scoffed at the reading, thanked me anyway, and went on his merry way.

Some time later, I found out that Mr. E did encounter problems, both at work and in his love life. Regarding the troubles at work, they were serious enough to cause him to lose his status as the golden boy of the company.

Sadly, he is still struggling to regain the respect of his corporate peers as well as attempting to win back his ex-fiancée.

Exercise 8—Troubled Woman

One lovely spring weekend I invited a few close girlfriends over to my house for a hen party and card reading session. I also encouraged each to bring along a girlfriend who might like to have her fortune told.

One of my friends was accompanied by a very pretty and quiet young woman. At first Ms. G demurred from having her fortune told, declaring she would be quite happy enough to watch.

But as the afternoon wore on, I could see how intrigued she was becoming by her friends' readings. She was especially impressed when one of the women exclaimed at the accuracy of the cards. Another woman agreed with her and confirmed the cards' infallibility by recounting how an earlier prediction for her had come true.

Seeing that her interest was piqued, the young woman's friend coaxed and encouraged her to allow her fortune to be read, and Ms. G finally gave in.

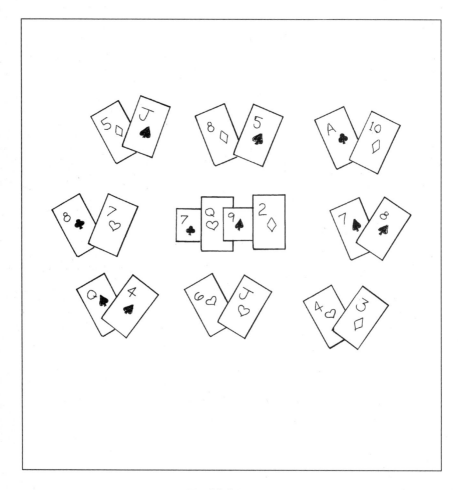

Troubled Woman

(Fifteen minutes later . . .)

It was no surprise when the cards revealed this woman had troubled experiences in her past. Friendships had suffered and, as a result, she'd wound up with little, if any, social life. Though she presently had a happy home environment, the arguments and jealousies she encountered affected her enough to make her ill at ease at meetings.

Moreover, Ms. G was emotionally distressed by someone trying to undermine her reputation.

The future the cards predicted for her was an interesting mix of situations and actions. The event most immediate showed her moving forward with ease and hope. There would be a nice gathering in store, where she could get her wish granted.

Interestingly enough, the cards also revealed the existence of a rival, yet that person's action would be doubtful.

Some weeks later we ran into each other. She was a changed woman and practically glowed with happiness. After I complimented her improved looks, she squeezed my hands and declared that it was thanks to the cards that she was happy once more. Until a short time before, she had been puzzled over why her friends had been increasingly shunning her company, but all was well now and she had regained her friends and nice social life.

Ms. G had discovered, to her surprise, that an acquaintance had been acting out of jealousy over her popularity. The latter had set out to blemish the young woman's reputation by spreading false rumors. Luckily, the Principal had been able to defend herself when the two women ran into each other at a party. In front of witnesses, the other woman's lies had finally caught up with her.

With the truth revealed, the other woman was asked to leave the gathering, and those people present, who had been taken in by her manipulative ways, sincerely apologized to Ms. G.

Parting Advice

I have to confess that, for purposes of comparison, I have sought out professionals to have my share of card readings done for me. Though their methods were different, some of the things they told me often coincided with what I'd read in my own layout.

What astounded me was that these people used the full deck in each layout. That means that each Principal would have all the good and bad things turn up at once.

I'm sure nobody objects to love, money, happiness, or travel, but who wants to see death, illness, tears, and failure in his or her future every time (or at all)? In my twenty-card Detailed Reading, many of the cards don't appear. So just as not everyone gets rich or happily married, neither does everybody have an impending death or grave illness in the family.

With my layouts, it is almost impossible to have two identical layouts ever. For example, take the numbers zero through nine and see how many different combinations you can create. You'll spend days, weeks, or even months and never see the end of it. Now imagine the fifty-two-card deck and how many different layouts are possible, especially when not all the cards are used in a single layout. The smallest layout, the Quick Cut, consists of only two cards.

The Detailed Reading's layout in this particular method of card fortune telling consists of twenty cards. Every time you spread those twenty cards in front of you, they (like different lives) will be in a different order.

That's where the art of reading comes in. Knowing the basic meaning of each card, you start connecting them and, according to their positions in the layout, you interpret them.

Be sure to express yourself in a neutral way. Don't go into descriptive detail like, "You'll meet a tall, dark, handsome Italian man [or woman]," which might never happen. But if you say, "You'll meet a man [or woman]" or, even better, "You'll meet a special man [or woman]" the chances are that event will take place and the romance may develop.

The same with money. Don't elaborate exactly where the money is coming from. Instead, hint at the possibility of a lottery win, a good business deal, a bargain purchase, or even finding a lucky penny on the street. Then the person won't be expecting a great inheritance when in fact he or she will only wind up with a 4 percent raise in salary.

Be especially subtle interpreting the tragedy cards. You don't want the Principal to panic or become unnecessarily concerned. For example, if you predict the death of an elderly woman close to the Principal, he or she may think of his or her mother, while in reality it is a coworker or a neighbor.

And never, never try to answer the questions like, "Will I get married?" or "Will I have children?" or "Will I have this or that?" There is no way you can answer such questions satisfactorily. Don't even lay the cards in answer to any questions. Instead, connect the Principal to the cards by letting him or her shuffle them. You simply read what is in the layout. If the answer is in the cards, he or she will get it. The cards will forecast what to expect and also tell what is actually happening in the life of the Principal.

But more than anything, don't do what most of the psychics do— don't ask questions trying to extract information from the Principal that will facilitate the reading!

In other words, don't be a charlatan.

Also, remember to have fun!

QUICK CARD SUIT REFERENCE TABLE

The following is a quick reference table that can easily be used as a tear sheet. It lists key words to help you, the apprentice Reader, recall individual cards' meanings while you are learning your new skill.

For more explicit descriptions of the cards, refer to chapter 2. You may recall that included in that chapter are examples of how an individual card's interpretation is influenced by the proximity of other cards.

	Diamond ◇	Spade ♠	Heart ♡	Club ♣	
King	Young man/ Son/Father	Rival/ Widower	Principal/ Male sweetheart/	Friendly older man/ Relation	King
Queen	Young woman/ Daughter/Mother	Rival/ Widow	Principal/ Female sweetheart/ Lady Luck	Friendly older woman/ Relation	Queen
Knight (Jack)	Expectation	Bad news/ Trouble	New hope/ Child	Friend	Knight (Jack)
10	Happiness	Big sorrow	Great joy	Money	10
9	Advice/Friendly surroundings/ Personal interest/ Ambition	Health problem/ Illness/ Funeral	Love/ Respect	Business site/ Enterprise	9
8	Socializing/ Pleasant talk	Argument	Friendly flirt	Job/ Business talk	8
7	Thoughts/ Wishful thinking/ Plans	Tears	Jealousy/ Envy	Worries	7
6	Steps	Failure/ Bad trip/ Unwise action	Very nice trip/Path	Business trip	6
5	Friendship	Loss	Small gift/ Little attention	Financial gain or loss	5
4	Decision/ Four corners	Doubtful/ Torn apart	Nice gathering	Financial insecurity/ Undecided business	4
3	Goal attained/ Success/ Wish granted	Cutoff/ Obstacle	You and only you	Perseverance/ Hard work	3
2	Meeting	Rift/ Breakup	Passion	Business meeting	2
Ace	News	Death/ Tragedy	Heart	Home	Ace

About the Author

Of Russian parentage, Chita St. Lawrence was born in Venezuela and raised and educated in California. Besides these places, she has lived at one time or another in Washington, D.C.; Austria; France; the Dominican Republic; and Bosnia.

Laughingly, she likes to declare: "I have moved around as much as any Gypsy!"

Fluent in several languages, she travels extensively, especially to Europe, where she has close family ties in Sarajevo. She holds a Bachelor of Science degree in oceanography.

Chita currently lives in New Jersey and loves scuba diving, fencing, horseback riding, and writing historical and modern romances.